Technical Trading Systems
for
Commodities and Stocks

by

Charles Patel

TRADERS PRESS™
INCORPORATED
P.O. BOX 6206
GREENVILLE, S.C. 29606

Books and Gifts
for Investors and Traders

ISBN: 0-934380-47-7

Reprinted by special arrangement.

Published August, 1998

DISCLAIMER

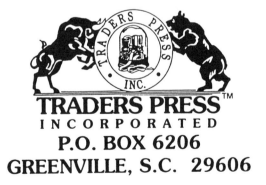

TRADERS PRESS™
INCORPORATED
P.O. BOX 6206
GREENVILLE, S.C. 29606

*Books and Gifts
for Investors and Traders*

*Tradersprs@aol.com
http://www.traderspress.com*

Acknowledgements

SPECIAL THANKS:

To ***Margaret Ros Hudson***
for her wonderful creative talents. She designed the beautiful cover for the reprint of this book.

To ***Teresa Darty Alligood***
for many hours of hard work in preparing this material for publication.

*To **Dennis D. Dunn***
for the inspiration to reprint this book.

From
Edward D. Dobson

FOREWORD

This superb collection of eighty-two technical trading systems will prove a valuable resource to traders and investors interested in a systematic technical approach to trading. It provides the formulas and the specific buy and sell rules for many well known (and many not so well known) systems in one easily read volume. Many Traders Press customers have called our office over the years looking for any material that would "shed light" on the methods of unpublished technicians such as Richard Donchian, and out of print authors such as Granville. This book should fill the need for a composite reference on the methods of many past technical analysts. Originally published in 1980, before the ready availability of backtesting software, no test results are shown herein. "Checking out" the current and past effectiveness of these methods should be a project of major interest to readers with the capability and inclination to do systems research and backtesting. If you are a reader that falls in this category, we at **Traders Press** would welcome your feedback on the results of your research.

It is our hope that making this out of print resource available again to the public will prove a worthwhile contribution to the present body of technical knowledge.

Edward D. Dobson
Traders Press, Inc.
Greenville, SC

August, 1998

INTRODUCTION

The investment approach presented in this book is strictly technical. The purpose of this book is to equip stock and commodity traders with new and already existing technical trading techniques to success in today's volatile markets.

Most of the books on Technical Analysis deal with commodities or with stocks. The author has endeavored to put in one book almost all existing technical techniques for trading stocks and commodities. Furthermore, the book includes the author's new and original trading methods based on his own personal research. These new Mechanical Methods are suitable for both trend-following strategies and trading-range applications.

The usual subject of Bar Chart and Point and Figure method is not discussed in this book.

All oscillators discussed herein can also be used for the generation of Buy and Sell signals at the zero line. When the oscillator crosses zero line on the upside, a Buy signal is generated and vice versa.

Price Filters and relative strength analysis don't lend themselves very well to Financial Futures.

Almost all the trading systems have been presented in the simplest form possible so that the beginner as well as the experienced trader can understand them. My aim is to be specific, not vague, so that anyone who follows the steps set forth in these systems will find it practical and easy to do Technical Analysis.

Application Guide, at the end of the book, describes in detail a practical and systematic approach to Technical Analysis. Specific guide lines are given for commodity trend, short/intermediate Term Stock trend and Long Term stock Trend for each system.

This book is addressed to any Technician/Investor/Trader who is interested in becoming more knowledgeable about Technical Analysis and who is prepared to have an open mind about it's applicability in the stock and commodity market.

A general apology is offered for any errors or omissions that may exist and suggestions and constructive criticisms are always welcomed.

Charles Patel

PREFACE

I have enjoyed working with you on your new book *Technical Trading Systems for Commodities and Stocks*. In my opinion, this well-researched book is a very important contribution to the literature on the stock and commodity futures markets. I feel privileged to have been a part of your education on technical trading methods and to have helped with the editing job for such a valuable book for investors.

Over the past few years, we have spent many hours discussing the concepts of technical trading systems. You have carefully compiled the most important techniques in a manner that is unique and refreshing——a brief and concise description of the system and how to calculate it. This book will become a handbook for market technicians which they in turn can turn to and quickly find the essence of each system without having to dig it out of vague obscure discussions which often leave you wondering how to actually determine the buy/sell signal.

The book is organized in such a way that an amateur investor can quickly read a chapter discussing how a trading system works and immediately calculate each value necessary to make the system work. The reader is taken step-by-step through each calculation so that even the most non-mathematical investor can repeat the process to determine the necessary information to make the system operative.

For the beginning student of technical analysis there is an extensive presentation of work sheets for every system which shows precise what data to collect and how to organize it in such a way that it is easy to calculate and meaningful to use. Very few books on the stock and commodities markets today have gone into such detail on how to determine specific buying and selling points for investing in stocks and commodities.

This book is written for the average investor who doesn't have a computer available to crunch huge amounts of data in order to printout stacks of paper with Betas, Alphas, etc. It is a book that gives a detailed description of do-it-yourself trading systems that can be applied with no more than an adding machine and slide rule or a ten-dollar pocket calculator. It's a How-To-Do book.

As you know, Dunn & Hargitt assembled the first complete Computer Database on commodity futures markets, we then tested all the available trading systems published in the literature using the computer at Purdue University. Because I have been researching technical trading systems on stocks and commodities for the past 20 years, and at one time or another I have tested almost all the concepts and systems described in this book (other than the author's original ideas), I can assure you that your book is packed with extremely profitable information.

To carry out our own research on trading systems, we had to dig out the specifics of each trading system from numerous books and now offer it all condensed into one convenient volume. From my many years of research on trading systems I have become familiar with most of the systems and techniques that have been published or have been used by market technicians both in commodities and stocks. Nevertheless, I have never seen a book that has compiled the basic formulae and calculation sheets necessary to do a large variety of technical analyses in a single, condensed publication. Therefore, I believe that every serious stock market investor has a need for your book.

Since 1962 I have been writing a weekly stock market advisory letter which has used certain of the formulae you describe in your book. Therefore, I can testify to the profitable weekly application of these systems over nearly 20 years of calling market trends. The Moving Average Trend following system we have employed in our advisory newsletter has called every significant market cycle since we started publication in March 1962. Few investment advisors can make and substantiate that claim which comes as a result of following trading systems like the ones you describe in your book.

Technical Trading Systems for Commodities and Stocks answers an important need for the formulae and specific buy/sell rules for various trading systems or methods in one easy-to-read reference volume. I have been reading the literature on the stock market and commodity futures markets for nearby 25 years. My experience tells me your book will be a great time-saver for the average investor who wants to understand technical analysis. Because of the wealth of information contained in the book it could sell for many times what you are asking and still be a bargain.

This book is <u>must reading</u> for every serious investor.

Edwin F. Hargitt
February, 1980

CONTENTS

SYSTEM I

SIMPLE MOVING AVERAGE

SYSTEM DEFINITIONS:

To calculate simple five day moving average,

1. Put daily closing prices in Col. I.

2. Add first five closing prices in Col. I and put the total in Col. 2,
    e.g., 26.50 + 26.00 + 25.00 + 25.25 + 25.13 = 127.88.

3. To calculate the moving total in line 6, Col. 2 add 25.00 (Line 6, Col. I)
    and subtract 26.50 (Line I, Col. I) from 127.88,
    e.g., 127.88 + 25.00 - 26.50 = 126.38.

4. Col. 3 = $\frac{\text{Col. 2}}{5}$ e.g., 25.27 = $\frac{126.38}{5}$

5. Buy signal is generated when the rising closing price penetrates the moving
    average on the upside.

6. Sell signal is generated when the falling closing price penetrates the moving
    average on the downside.

7. When a new Buy or Sell signal is generated, the old position is liquidated
    simultaneously. In other words, the system keeps you in the market all the
    time.

DISCUSSION OF THE SYSTEM:

There are three major criticisms of the simple moving average.

1. It assigns equal weight to all readings, e.g., for a ten day moving average,
    each day is assigned 10% weight.

2. The moving average is dependent on two numbers - the one being added and
    the other being subtracted. If the number to be added is larger than the
    number to be subtracted, the moving average increases and vice versa.

3. Data bank for previous readings should be maintained, e.g., if we are working
    with 30 day simple moving average, we should maintain previous thirty
    readings.

1

WORK SHEET

SYSTEM I

SIMPLE MOVING AVERAGE

	1 Daily Closing Price	2 5 Day Simple Moving Total of Col. 1	3 5 Day Simple Moving Average of Col. 1	
1	26.50			
2	26.00			
3	25.00			
4	25.25			
5	25.13	127.88	25.58	
6	25.00	126.38	25.27	
7	(25.25)	125.63	(25.13)	Since the closing price of 25.25 penetrates the moving average of 25.13 on the upside, a Buy signal is generated.
8	25.50	126.13	25.23	
9	25.63	126.51	25.30	
10	25.75	127.13	25.43	
11	25.55	127.68	25.54	
12	26.00	128.43	25.69	
13	26.50	129.43	25.89	
14	27.00	130.80	26.16	
15	27.50	132.55	26.51	
16	27.25	134.25	26.85	Since the closing price of 27.00 penetrates the moving average of 27.05 on the downside, a Sell signal is generated.
17	(27.00)	135.28	(27.05)	
18	26.75	135.50	27.10	
19	26.50	135.00	27.00	
20	26.20	135.70	26.74	
21	25.20	131.65	26.33	

SYSTEM 2

EXPONENTIALLY SMOOTHED MOVING AVERAGE

SYSTEM DEFINITIONS:

To calculate 5 day Exponentially Smoothed moving average,

1. Put daily closing prices in Col. 1.

2. To start, add first five closing prices in Col. 1 and put five day simple moving average in Col. 2, e.g., 26.50 + 26.00 + 25.00 + 25.25 + 25.13 = 127.88, then $\frac{127.88}{5} = 25.58$

3. Exponential constant or smoothing constant = $\frac{2}{n+1}$ where n = time period of moving average.

    For a 5 day time period, Exponential constant = $\frac{2}{n+1}$ = $\frac{2}{5+1}$

    = $\frac{2}{6}$ = 0.33

4. New ESMA = (Closing Price - Old ESMA) X .33 + old ESMA

    e.g., 25.39 = (25.00 - 25.58) X .33 + 25.58

                                    or

    New ESMA = Closing Price X (.33) + old ESMA X (1- .33)

    e.g., 25.39 = 25.00 X (.33) + 25.58 X (1- .33) = 25.00 X (.33) +25.58 X (.67)

    Put this value in Col. 2.

5. Buy signal is generated when the rising closing price penetrates the moving average on the upside.

6. Sell signal is generated when the falling closing price penetrates the moving average on the downside.

7. When a new Buy or Sell signal is generated, the old position is liquidated simultaneously. In other words, the system stays in the market all the time.

DISCUSSION OF THE SYSTEM:

1. Assigns .33 to the closing price and remaining .67 to the previous moving average.

2. One form of weighted moving average.

3. Much easier to calculate.

4. Requires less time to update.

5. Requires smoothing constant and previous ESMA.

WORK SHEET

SYSTEM 2

EXPONENTIALLY SMOOTHED
MOVING AVERAGE

	1 Daily Closing Price	2 5 Day Exponentially Smoothed Moving Average of Col. 1	
1	26.50		
2	26.00		
3	25.00		
4	25.25		
5	25.13	25.58	
6	25.00	25.39	
7	25.25	25.34	
8	(25.50)	(25.39)	Since the closing price of 25.50 penetrates the moving average of 25.39 on the upside, a Buy Signal is generated.
9	25.63	25.47	
10	25.75	25.56	
11	25.55	25.56	
12	26.00	25.71	
13	26.50	25.97	
14	27.00	26.31	
15	27.50	26.70	
16	27.25	26.88	
17	27.00	26.92	
18	(26.75)	(26.86)	Since the closing price of 26.75 penetrates the moving average of 26.86 on the downside, a Sell signal is generated.
19	26.50	26.74	
20	26.20	26.56	
21	25.20	26.11	

Formula:

New ESMA = (Closing Price - old ESMA) X (.33) + old ESMA

or

New ESMA = Closing Price X (.33) + old ESMA X (1-0.33)

SMOOTHING CONSTANTS FOR EXPONENTIALLY SMOOTHED MOVING AVERAGE

No. of Days	Smoothing Constant	No. of Days	Smoothing Constant	No. of Days	Smoothing Constant	No. of Days	Smoothing Constant	No. of Days	Smoothing Constant
1	1.0000	31	.0625	61	.0323	91	.0217	121	.0164
2	.6667	32	.0606	62	.0317	92	.0215	122	.0163
3	.5000	33	.0588	63	.0313	93	.0213	123	.0161
4	.4000	34	.0571	64	.0308	94	.0211	124	.0160
5	.3333	35	.0556	65	.0303	95	.0208	125	.0159
6	.2857	36	.0541	66	.0299	96	.0206	126	.0157
7	.2500	37	.0526	67	.0294	97	.0204	127	.0156
8	.2222	38	.0513	68	.0290	98	.0202	128	.0155
9	.2000	39	.0500	69	.0286	99	.0200	129	.0154
10	.1818	40	.0488	70	.0282	100	.0198	130	.0153
11	.1667	41	.0476	71	.0278	101	.0196	131	.0152
12	.1538	42	.0465	72	.0274	102	.0194	132	.0150
13	.1429	43	.0455	73	.0270	103	.0192	133	.0149
14	.1333	44	.0444	74	.0267	104	.0190	134	.0148
15	.1250	45	.0435	75	.0263	105	.0189	135	.0147
16	.1176	46	.0426	76	.0260	106	.0187	136	.0146
17	.1111	47	.0417	77	.0256	107	.0185	137	.0145
18	.1053	48	.0408	78	.0253	108	.0183	138	.0144
19	.1000	49	.0400	79	.0250	109	.0182	139	.0143
20	.0952	50	.0392	80	.0247	110	.0180	140	.0142
21	.0909	51	.0385	81	.0244	111	.0179	141	.0141
22	.0870	52	.0377	82	.0241	112	.0177	142	.0140
23	.0833	53	.0370	83	.0238	113	.0175	143	.0139
24	.0800	54	.0364	84	.0235	114	.0174	144	.0138
25	.0769	55	.0357	85	.0233	115	.0172	145	.0137
26	.0741	56	.0351	86	.0230	116	.0171	146	.0136
27	.0714	67	.0345	87	.0227	117	.0169	147	.0135
28	.0690	58	.0339	88	.0225	118	.0168	148	.0134
29	.0667	59	.0333	89	.0222	119	.0167	149	.0133
30	.0645	60	.0328	90	.0220	120	.0165	150	.0132

Formula:

Smoothing Constant $= \dfrac{2}{n+1}$ Where n = time period (i.e. No. of Days)

SYSTEM 3

STEP WEIGHTED MOVING AVERAGE

SYSTEM DEFINITIONS:

To calculate five day step weighted Moving Average,

1. Put daily closing prices in Col. 1.

2. In Col. 2, put Weights 1, 2, 3, 4, and 5 for the first five closing prices. Then, use 5 for the remainder of the closing prices.

3. Col. 3 = Col. 1 X Col. 2

4. Add first five numbers in Col. 3 and put the total in Col. 5

    e.g., 26.50 + 52.00 + 75.00 + 101.00 + 125.65 = 380.15

5. Add five previous Closing Prices excluding today and put the total in Col. 4.

6. Col. 5 is the 5 day step weighted moving total.

New 5 day Step Weighted Moving Total	=	Previous 5 day Step Weighted Moving Total	+	Current Price X 5 (Col.3)	-	Sum of five Previous Closing Prices excluding Today (Col. 4)

Or

Using the most recent set of 5 days as 5th day, 4th day, 3rd day, 2nd day and today,

New 5 day step weighted Moving Total = Today's close X 5 + 2nd day's Close X 4 + 3rd day's Close X 3 + 4th day's Close X 2 + 5th day's Close x 1

7. $\text{Col. 6} = \dfrac{\text{Col. 5}}{1+2+3+4+5} = \dfrac{\text{Col. 5}}{15}$

8. Buy Signal is generated when the rising Closing price penetrates the Moving Average on the upside.

9. Sell Signal is generated when the falling Closing price penetrates the Moving Average on the downside.

10. When a new Buy or Sell signal is generated, the old position is liquidated simultaneously. In other words, the system is always in the market.

DISCUSSION OF THE SYSTEM:

1. Assigns greater weight to most recent readings and lesser weight to the older readings, e.g., assigns 5 to the most recent reading, 4 to the reading before and so on.

2. Cumbersome to do calculations by hand.

3. Computer or sophisticated calculator simplifies the calculations.

WORK SHEET

SYSTEM 3

STEP WEIGHTED MOVING AVERAGE

	1 Daily Closing Price	2 Weights	3 Daily Close X Weight	4 Sum of five previous Closing Prices Excluding Today	5 5 Day Step Weighted Moving Total	6 5 Day Step Weighted Moving Average = Col 5 / 15	
1	26.50	1	26.50				
2	26.00	2	52.00				
3	25.00	3	75.00				
4	25.25	4	101.00				
5	25.13	5	125.65		380.15	25.34	
6	25.00	5	125.00	127.88	377.27	25.15	
7	(25.25)	5	126.25	126.38	377.14	(25.14)	Since the closing price of 25.25 penetrates the moving average of 25.14 on the upside, a Buy signal is generated.
8	25.50	5	127.50	125.63	379.01	25.27	
9	25.63	5	128.15	126.13	381.03	25.40	
10	25.75	5	128.75	126.51	383.27	25.55	
11	25.70	5	128.50	127.13	384.64	25.64	
12	26.00	5	130.00	127.83	386.81	25.79	
13	26.50	5	132.50	128.58	390.73	26.05	
14	27.00	5	135.00	129.58	396.15	26.41	
15	27.50	5	137.50	130.95	402.70	26.85	
16	27.25	5	136.25	132.70	406.25	27.08	
17	(27.00)	5	135.00	134.25	407.00	(27.13)	Since the closing price of 27.00 penetrates the moving average of 27.13 on the downside, a Sell signal is generated.
18	26.75	5	133.75	135.25	405.50	27.03	

7

SYSTEM 4

LINEARLY STEP WEIGHTED MOVING AVERAGE

SYSTEM DEFINITIONS:

To calculate six day linearly step weighted moving average,

(1)   Put daily closing prices in Col. 1.

(2)   In Col. 2, put Weights 1, 1, 2, 2, 3, and 3 for the first six closing prices. Then, use 3 for the remainder of the closing prices.

(3)   Col. 3 = Col. 1 X Col. 2

(4)   Add first six numbers in Col. 3 and put the total in Col. 5

     e.g., 26.50 + 26.00 + 50.00 + 50.50 + 75.39 + 75.00 = 303.39

(5)   Add six previous Closing Prices excluding today, divide by two and put the Value in Col. 4.

(6)   Col. 5 is the 6 day linearly step weighted moving total.

$$\begin{array}{llllll}
\text{New 6 day linearly} & & \text{Previous 6 day} & & \text{Current Price} & \text{Sum of six} \\
\text{Step Weighted} & = & \text{linearly Step} & + & \text{X} & - \;\text{Previous Closing} \\
\text{Moving Total} & & \text{Weighted Moving} & & 3 & \text{Prices excluding} \\
 & & \text{Total} & & \text{(Col.3)} & \text{Today (Col. 4)} \\
 & & & & & \div \\
 & & & & & 2
\end{array}$$

Or

Using the most recent set of 6 days as 6th day, 5th day, 4th day, 3rd day, 2nd day and today,

New 6 day linearly step weighted
Moving Total   = Today's close X 6 + 2nd day's Close X 5
+ 3rd day's Close X 4 + 4th day's Close
X 3 + 5th day's Close X 2 + 6th day's Close X 1

(7)   Col. 6 $= \dfrac{\text{Col. 5}}{1+1+2+2+3+3} = \dfrac{\text{Col. 5}}{12}$

(8)   Buy Signal is generated when the rising Closing price penetrates the Moving Average on the upside.

(9)   Sell Signal is generated when the falling Closing price penetrates the moving average on the downside.

(10)   When a new Buy or Sell signal is generated, the old position is liquidated simultaneously. In other words, the system is always in the market.

DISCUSSION OF THE SYSTEM:

(1)   This is basically the same system as step weighted moving average. Instead of assigning the weights: 1, 2, 3, 4, 5, and 6, the weights assigned are linear: 1, 1, 2, 2, 3 and 3.

(2)   Since the weights assigned are linear, simplifies the calculations by hand to some extent.

(3)   Computer or sophisticated calculator simplifies the calculations.

WORK SHEET

SYSTEM 4

LINEARLY STEP WEIGHTED MOVING AVERAGE

	1 Daily Closing Price	2 Linear Weights	3 Daily Close X Linear Weight	4 Sum of Six previous Closings Excluding Today ÷ 2	5 6 Day Linearly Step Weighted Moving Total	6 6 Day Linearly Step Weighted Moving Average = Col 5 / 12	
1	26.50	1	26.50				
2	26.00	1	26.00				
3	25.00	2	50.00				
4	25.25	2	50.50				
5	25.13	3	75.39				
6	25.00	3	75.00		303.39	25.28	
7	(25.25)	3	75.75	76.44	302.70	(25.23)	Since the closing price of 25.25 penetrates the moving average of 25.23 on the upside, a Buy signal is generated.
8	25.50	3	76.50	75.82	303.38	25.28	
9	25.63	3	76.89	75.57	304.70	25.39	
10	25.75	3	77.25	75.88	306.07	25.51	
11	25.70	3	77.10	76.13	307.40	25.59	
12	26.00	3	78.00	76.42	308.62	25.72	
13	26.50	3	79.50	76.92	311.20	25.93	
14	27.00	3	81.00	77.54	314.66	26.22	
15	27.50	3	82.50	78.29	318.87	26.57	
16	27.25	3	81.75	79.23	321.39	26.78	
17	27.00	3	81.00	79.98	322.41	26.87	
18	(26.75)	3	80.25	80.63	322.03	(26.84)	Since the closing price of 26.75 penetrates the moving average of 26.84 on the downside, a Sell signal is generated.

SYSTEM 5

SINGLE MOVING AVERAGE WITH TIME FILTER

SYSTEM DEFINITIONS:

Suppose we are working with 39 day exponentially smoothed moving average. Then,

(1)   Put daily closing prices in Col. 1.

(2)   To start, add first 39 closing prices in Col. 1, divide by 39 and put in Col. 2.

(3)   Smoothing constant $= \dfrac{2}{n+1} = \dfrac{2}{39+1} = .05$

(4)   New ESMA = (Closing Price - old ESMA) X .05 + old ESMA.

$$\text{Or}$$

New ESMA = Closing Price X (.05) + Old ESMA X (1- .05)

Put this value in Col. 2.

(5)   Buy signal is generated when the closing price penetrates the moving average on the upside and stays above moving average for any five days (Provided the slope of the moving average is positive, i.e. moving average increases every day).

(6)   Sell signal is generated when the closing price penetrates the moving average on the downside and stays below moving average for any five days (Provided the slope of the moving average is negative, i.e. moving average decreases every day).

(7)   When a new Buy or Sell signal is generated, the old position is liquidated simultaneously. In other words, the system is always in the market.

DISCUSSION OF THE SYSTEM:

(1)   Since we are using the benefit of a time filter to confirm the trend reversal, this will reduce some of the false Buy and Sell signals in the trading range.

(2)   Works very well for strong stocks and commodities.

WORK SHEET

SYSTEM 5

SINGLE MOVING AVERAGE
WITH TIME FILTER

	1 Daily Closing	2 39 Day Exponentially Smoothed Moving Average of Col. 1	
1		36.05	Sum of 39 Previous closing prices (not shown) ÷ 39
2	36.00	36.05	
3	(36.25)	(36.05)	First Buy signal (since 36.25 penetrated 36.05 on the upside)
4	(36.50)	36.08	
5	(36.25)	36.09	
6	(36.75)	36.12	
7	(37.00)	(36.17)	Confirmed Buy Signal
8	37.50	36.25	Since 36.25, 36.50, 36.25, 36.75 and 37.00 stays above the moving average for any five days, we have a confirmed Buy signal.
9	38.00	36.32	
10	37.00	36.35	
11	39.50	36.51	
12	40.00	36.69	

SYSTEM 6

SINGLE MOVING AVERAGE WITH PRICE FILTER

SYSTEM DEFINITIONS:

Suppose we are working with 39 day exponentially smoothed moving average, then

(1)   Put daily closing prices in Col. I.

(2)   To start, add first 39 closing prices in Col. I, divide by 39 and put in Col. 2.

(3)   Smoothing constant $= \dfrac{2}{n+1} = \dfrac{2}{39+1} = \dfrac{2}{40} = .05$

(4)   New ESMA = (Closing Price - old ESMA) X .05 + old ESMA

Or

New ESMA = Closing Price X (.05) + Old ESMA (1- .05)

Put this value in Col. 2.

(5)   Buy signal is generated when the closing price penetrates the moving average on the upside by

6%	for below $20
5%	for $20 to $39
4%	for $40 to $59
3%	for $60 to $199
2%	for over $199 (Provided the slope of the moving average is positive, i.e. moving average increases)

(6)   Sell signal is generated when the closing price penetrates the moving average on the downside by

6%	for below $20
5%	for $20 to $39
4%	for $40 to $59
3%	for $60 to $199
2%	for over $199 (Provided the slope of the moving average is negative, i.e. moving average decreases)

(7)   When a new Buy or Sell signal is generated, the old position is liquidated simultaneously. In other words, the system keeps you in the market all the time.

DISCUSSION OF THE SYSTEM:

(1)   Since we are using a price filter to confirm the trend reversal, this will reduce some of the false Buy and Sell signals during the trading range.

WORK SHEET

SYSTEM 6

SINGLE MOVING AVERAGE WITH PRICE FILTER

	1 Daily Closing Price	2 39 Day Exponentially Smoothed Moving Average of Col. 1
1		36.05
2	36.00	36.05
3	36.25	36.06
4	36.50	36.08
5	36.25	36.09
6	36.75	36.12
7	37.00	36.17
8	37.50	36.25
9	38.00	36.32
10	37.00	36.35
11	(39.50)	36.51

36.05 ◁———— Sum of 39 previous closing prices (not shown) ÷ 39

Price		Moving Average		Penetration
36.25	÷	36.06	=	.52%
36.50	÷	36.08	=	1.16%
36.25	÷	36.09	=	.44%
36.75	÷	36.12	=	1.74%
37.00	÷	36.17	=	2.29%
37.50	÷	36.25	=	3.45%
38.00	÷	36.32	=	4.62%
37.00	÷	36.35	=	1.79%
39.50	÷	36.51	=	(8.18%)

No Buy Signal generated since the penetration is less than 5%.

Buy signal generated since the penetration is more than 5%.

13

SYSTEM 7

SINGLE MOVING AVERAGE WITH VOLATILITY FILTER

SYSTEM DEFINITIONS:

(1)   Put daily closing prices in Col. 1.

(2)   To start, add first 39 closing prices in Col. 1, divide by 39 and put in Col. 2.

(3)   Smoothing constant $= \dfrac{2}{n+1} = \dfrac{2}{39+1} = \dfrac{2}{40} = .05$

(4)   New ESMA = (Closing price - old ESMA) X .05 + old ESMA

Or

New ESMA =   Closing Price X (.05) + Old ESMA (1- .05)

Put this value in Col. 2.

(5)   Buy signal is generated when the closing price penetrates the moving average on the upside by 8 week average of the price range.

(6)   Sell Signal is generated when the closing price penetrates the moving average on the downside by 8 week average of the price range.

(7)   When a new Buy or Sell signal is generated, the old position is liquidated simultaneously. In other words, the system keeps you in the market all the time.

DISCUSSION OF THE SYSTEM:

(1)   This system is almost the same as the price filter system. But, instead of using x% penetration for y dollars, we are using the volatility of the stock/commodity during 39 day time period. 39 days $\cong$ 8 weeks. To calculate the volatility, we can use weekly prices instead of daily prices as follows: e.g.,

Time	High	Low	Range
Week 1	36.00	35.00	1.00
Week 2	36.00	34.50	1.50
Week 3	36.50	35.00	1.50
Week 4	37.00	35.00	2.00
Week 5	37.50	36.00	1.50
Week 6	38.00	36.50	1.50
Week 7	38.50	36.50	2.00
Week 8	39.00	37.00	2.00

$$\text{Volatility Filter} = \frac{1.00 + 1.50 + 1.50 + 2.00 + 1.50 + 1.50 + 2.00 + 2.00}{8} = \frac{13}{8} = 1.63$$

i.e., Buy signal is generated when the closing price penetrates the   moving average on the upside by 1.63 and vice versa.

14

WORK SHEET

SYSTEM 7

SINGLE MOVING AVERAGE WITH VOLATILITY FILTER

	1 Daily Closing Price	2 39 Day Exponentially Smoothed Moving Average of Col. 1						
		36.05	← Sum of 39 previous closing prices (not shown) ÷ 39					
2	36.00	36.05	Price		Moving Average		Penetration	
3	36.25	36.06	36.25	−	36.06	=	.19	No Buy Signal
4	36.50	36.08	36.50	−	36.08	=	.42	generated since
5	36.25	36.09	36.25	−	36.09	=	.16	← the penetration
6	36.75	36.12	36.75	−	36.12	=	.63	is less than 1.63.
7	37.00	36.17	37.00	−	36.17	=	.83	
8	37.50	36.25	37.50	−	36.25	=	1.25	
9	(38.00)	36.32	38.00	−	36.32	=	(1.68)	← Buy signal gen- erated since the penetration is more than 1.63.
10	37.00	36.35						
11	39.50	36.51						
12	40.00	36.69						

SYSTEM 8

SINGLE MOVING AVERAGE WITH TIME AND PRICE FILTER

SYSTEM DEFINITIONS:

Suppose we are working with 39 day exponentially smoothed moving average, Then

(1)   Put daily closing prices in Col. I.

(2)   To start, add first 39 closing prices in Col. I, divide by 39 and put in Col. 2.

(3)   Smoothing constant $= \dfrac{2}{n+1} = \dfrac{2}{39+1} = \dfrac{2}{40} = .05$

(4)   New ESMA = (Closing Price - old ESMA) X .05 + old ESMA

Or

New ESMA = Closing Price X (.05) + Old ESMA (1- .05)

Put this value in Col. 2.

(5)   Buy signal is generated when the closing price penetrates the moving average on the upside and stays above moving average for any five days with a single penetration of

6%	for below $20
5%	for $20 to $39
4%	for $40 to $59
3%	for $60 to $199
2%	for over $199 (Provided the slope of the moving average is positive, i.e. moving average increases)

(6)   Sell signal is generated when the closing price penetrates the moving average on the downside and stays below the moving average for any five days with a single penetration of

6%	for below $20
5%	for $20 to $39
4%	for $40 to $59
3%	for $60 to $199
2%	for over $199 (Provided the slope of the moving average is negative, i.e. moving average decreases)

(7)   When a new Buy or Sell signal is generated, the old position is liquidated simultaneously. In other words, the system keeps you in the market all the time.

DISCUSSION OF THE SYSTEM:

(1)   Since we are using the benefit of both time and price filters to confirm the trend reversal, this will reduce most of the false buy and sell signals during the trading range. Out of all techniques using a moving average, this is one of the best. Basic limitations of a moving average are discussed in System 17.

WORK SHEET

SYSTEM 8

SINGLE MOVING AVERAGE WITH TIME AND PRICE FILTER

	1 Daily Closing	2 39 Day Exponentially Smoothed Moving Average of Col. 1
1		36.05
2	36.00	36.05
3	36.25	36.06
4	36.50	36.08
5	36.25	36.09
6	36.75	36.12
7	37.00	36.17
8	37.50	36.25
9	38.00	36.32
10	37.00	36.35
11	(39.50)	36.51
12	40.00	36.69

Sum of previous 39 Closing prices (not shown) ÷ 39

Price		Moving Average		Penetration
36.25	÷	36.06	=	0.52%
36.50	÷	36.08	=	1.16%
36.25	÷	36.09	=	0.44%
36.75	÷	36.12	=	1.74%
37.00	÷	36.17	=	2.29%
37.50	÷	36.25	=	3.45%
38.00	÷	36.32	=	4.62%
37.00	÷	36.35	=	1.79%
39.50	÷	36.51	=	(8.18%)

Buy signal generated by Time Filter since closing price stays above moving average for any five days. But no Buy signal is generated since the penetration is less than 5%.

Buy signal generated since the closing price stays above moving average for any five days and the penetration is more than 5%.

SYSTEM 9

MOVING AVERAGE TO PROJECT CHANNEL

SYSTEM DEFINITIONS:

(1)   Put Weekly High Price in Col. 1.

(2)   Put Weekly Low Price in Col. 2.

(3)   Put Weekly Close Price in Col. 3.

(4)   To start, add first 10 closing prices, divide by 10 and put in Col. 4.

(5)   Using a smoothing constant $\dfrac{2}{n+1} = \dfrac{2}{10+1} = \dfrac{2}{11} = .18$

(6)   New ESMA = (Closing price - old ESMA) x .18 + old ESMA

$$Or$$

New ESMA = Closing price X (.18) + old ESMA (1- .18)

(7)   Put this ESMA price in Col. 4. ESMA is based on closing price.

(8)   Plot this 10 week moving average with 5 week lag or plot 10 week centered moving average

(9)   Create a channel around the centered moving average.

(10)   Stock or commodity will oscillate within the bounds of the channel.

(11)   Buy signal can be acted upon when the price reaches the lower channel.

(12)   Sell signal can be acted upon when the price reaches the upper channel.

(13)   When a new Buy or Sell signal is generated, the old position is liquidated simultaneously. In other words, the system stays in the market all the time.

WORK SHEET

SYSTEM 9

MOVING AVERAGE TO PROJECT CHANNEL

	1 Weekly High Price	2 Weekly Low Price	3 Weekly Close Price	4 10 Week Exponentially Smoothed Moving Average of Col. 3	
1				36.78 ◁	Sum of 10
2	37.50	37.13	37.30	36.87	closing pri-
3	37.28	36.90	37.10	36.91	ces (not
4	37.10	36.85	37.00	36.93	shown)÷10
5	37.00	36.65	36.80	36.91	
6	36.75	36.50	36.50	36.83	
7	36.50	36.25	36.35	36.75	
8	36.70	36.45	36.60	36.72	
9	37.00	36.70	36.90	36.75	
10	37.30	37.10	37.20	36.83	
11	37.60	37.30	37.40	36.94	
12	37.70	37.50	37.60	37.05	
13	37.80	37.50	37.60	37.15	
14	37.60	37.35	37.47	37.21	
15	37.40	37.20	37.30	37.23	
16	37.30	37.10	37.20	37.22	
17	37.25	37.05	37.13	37.20	
18	37.15	36.95	37.10	37.19	
19	37.20	37.00	37.10	37.17	
20	37.35	37.15	37.30	37.19	
21	37.60	37.40	37.50	37.25	
22	37.85	37.65	37.70	37.33	
23	38.05	37.80	37.90	37.43	
24	38.25	38.05	38.20	37.57	
25	38.50	38.30	38.30	37.70	
26	38.65	38.50	38.60	37.86	
27	39.00	38.70	38.90	38.05	

SYSTEM 9

MOVING AVERAGE TO PROJECT CHANNEL

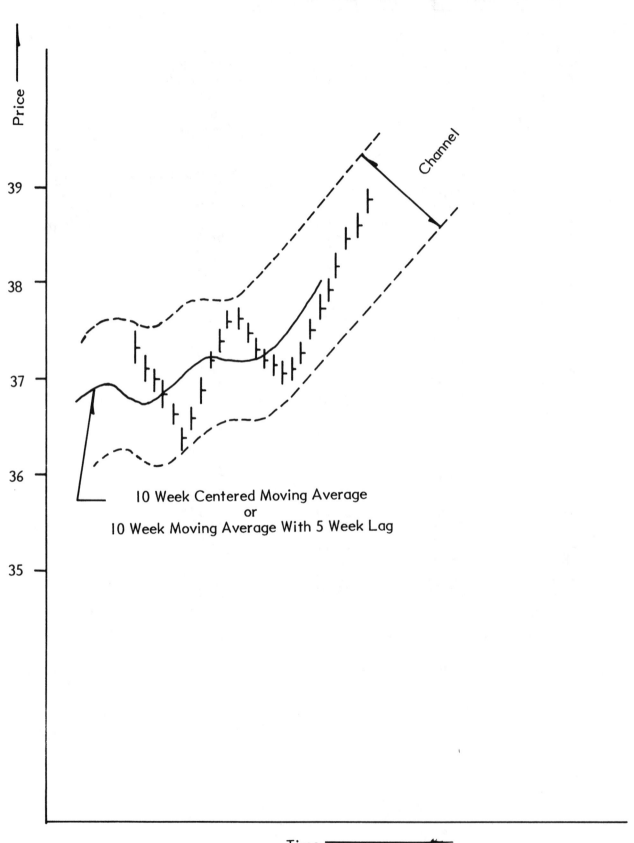

Price

Time

39

38

37

36

35

Channel

10 Week Centered Moving Average
or
10 Week Moving Average With 5 Week Lag

20

SYSTEM 10

MOVING AVERAGE - LARRY WILLIAMS' SHADOW LINE

SYSTEM DEFINITIONS:

(1)   Put weekly closing prices in Col. 1.

(2)   To start, add first 10 closing prices, divide by 10 and put in Col. 2.

(3)   Using a smoothing constant $\dfrac{2}{n+1}$ = $\dfrac{2}{10+1}$ = $\dfrac{2}{11}$ = .18,

(4)   New ESMA = (Closing Price - old ESMA) X .18 + old ESMA

                    Or

        New ESMA = Closing price X (.18) + old ESMA (1- .18)

        Put this ESMA price in Col. 2.

(5)   Plot this 10 week moving average coincident (no lag or lead) with closing price. (Solid Line on Chart)

(6)   Plot the same 10 week moving average with one week lead, called the shadow line. (Dotted line on chart)

(7)   Buy signal is generated when the moving average crosses its shadow line from below to above.

(8)   Sell signal is generated when the moving average crosses its shadow line from above to below.

(9)   When a new Buy or Sell signal is generated, the old position is liquidated simultaneously. In other words, the system stays in the market all the time.

DISCUSSION OF THE SYSTEM:

(1)   Completely mechanical method of trading.

(2)   Results are very encouraging.

(3)   Works very well with strongly trended stocks and commodities.

(4)   Avoids whipsaws during trading range.

(5)   Profitable trades during uptrend and downtrend.

WORK SHEET

SYSTEM 10

MOVING AVERAGE - LARRY WILLIAMS' SHADOW LINE

	1 Weekly Closing Price	2 10 Week Exponentially Smoothed Moving Average of Col. 1	
1		34.88	Sum of 10 Clos-ing prices (not shown) ÷10
2	37.50	35.35	
3	38.08	35.84	
4	37.17	36.08	
5	39.00	36.61	
6	36.75	36.63	
7	35.13	36.36	
8	36.00	36.30	
9	36.25	36.29	
10	35.75	36.19	
11	35.75	36.11	
12	37.75	36.41	
13	38.25	36.74	
14	35.00	36.43	
15	35.50	36.26	
16	35.00	36.03	
17	36.38	36.10	
18	36.50	36.17	
19	36.25	36.18	
20	36.75	36.28	
21	36.00	36.23	
22	35.00	36.01	
23	34.50	35.74	
24	32.75	35.20	
25	33.00	34.81	
26	34.25	34.71	
27	34.50	34.67	
28	35.25	34.77	
29	36.75	35.13	
30	35.25	35.15	

SYSTEM 10

MOVING AVERAGE-LARRY WILLIAMS' SHADOW LINE

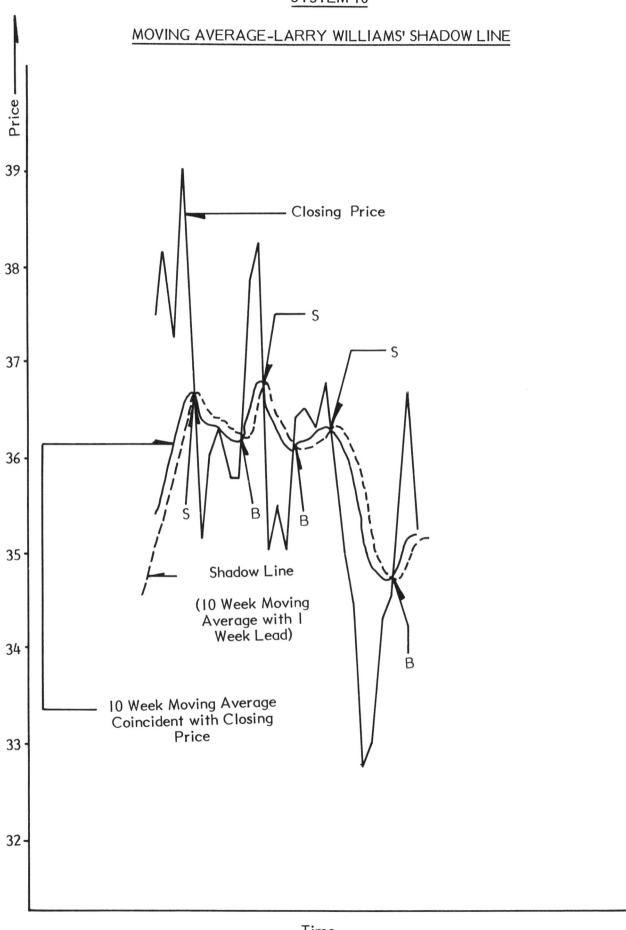

METHOD OF MEASURING CYCLE'S MOMENTUM
USING CONSISTENT MOVING AVERAGE

GENERAL THEORY AND DISCUSSION:

(1) Collect High, Low and close price on weekly basis for last six to nine months for the stock or commodity of your interest.

(2) Plot the data using weekly Bar Charts.

(3) Measure the distance from top to top and let it be $T_1, T_2, T_3 \ldots \ldots T_n$.

(4) Measure the distance from bottom to bottom and let it be $B_1, B_2, B_3 \ldots B_n$.

(5) Then consistent moving average length for

$$n = 4 \text{ is } \frac{T_1 + T_2 + T_3 + T_4 + B_1 + B_2 + B_3 + B_4}{8}$$

(6) For our example, $T_1 = 9 \quad T_2 = 10 \quad T_3 = 11 \text{ and } T_4 = 10$

$$B_1 = 8 \quad B_2 = 12 \quad B_3 = 10 \text{ and } B_4 = 10$$

(7) Then consistent moving average length $= \dfrac{9 + 10 + 11 + 10 + 8 + 12 + 10 + 10}{8} = 10$
Therefore, we will be using 10 week moving average.

(8) Rate of change (RC) = ½ moving average length $= \dfrac{10}{2} = 5$.

So we will be using rate of change 5 weeks ago.

(9) Since we are measuring cycle's momentum using consistent moving average length, Buy and Sell signals will be generally very good.

(10) Be cautious when the oscillator becomes extremely overbought or oversold.

(11) Works very well for stocks as well as commodities.

SYSTEM II

Continued

SYSTEM DEFINITIONS:

(1)   Put weekly closing prices in Col. I.

(2)   To start, add first 10 closing prices, divide by 10 and put in Col. 2.

(3)   Using a smoothing constant $= \dfrac{2}{n+1} = \dfrac{2}{10+1} = \dfrac{2}{11} = .18$

(4)   New ESMA = (Closing price - old ESMA) X .18 + old ESMA

                                     or

New ESMA = closing price x (.18) + old ESMA (1 - .18)

Put this ESMA price in Col. 2.

(5)   Rate of change 5 weeks ago (RC 5).

$$= \frac{\text{Moving Average this week - Moving Avg. 5 weeks ago}}{\text{Moving Avg. 5 weeks ago}}$$

(6)   Sell signal is generated when the oscillator tops-out (successive higher readings followed by lower reading) Provide the oscillator reversal point is in the positive territory, e.g., 1.20, 1.25, 1.30, 1.35 1.40 1.37.

(7)   Buy signal is generated when the oscillator bottoms-out (successive lower readings followed by a higher reading) provided the oscillator reversal point is in the negative territory, e.g., -1.20, -1.30, -1.40, -1.60, -1.90 -.05.

(8)   When a new Buy or Sell signal is generated, the old position is liquidated simultaneously. In other words, the system will keep you in the market all the time.

WORK SHEET

SYSTEM II

METHOD OF MEASURING CYCLE'S MOMENTUM

USING MOVING AVERAGE

	1 Weekly Closing Price	2 10 Week Exponentially Smoothed Moving Average of Col. 1	3 RC 5 Oscillator based on Col. 2	
1		45.99		
2	46.00	45.99		
3	46.25	46.04		
4	46.75	46.17		
5	47.25	46.36		
6	48.00	46.66	1.46	
7	47.00	46.72	1.59	
8	48.50	47.04	2.17	
9	49.75	47.53	2.95	
10	50.25	48.02	3.58	
11	50.75	48.51	3.96	
12	51.00	48.96	4.79	Top
13	(49.00)	48.97	(4.10)	Sell
14	49.00	48.98	3.05	
15	48.00	48.80	1.62	
16	47.50	48.57	.12	
17	46.00	48.11	-1.74	
18	45.50	47.64	-2.72	
19	44.75	47.12	-3.80	
20	44.00	46.56	-4.59	
21	44.00	46.09	-5.11	Bottom
22	(44.50)	45.80	(-4.80)	Buy
23	44.75	45.61	-4.26	

MEASURING CYCLE'S MOMENTUM USING CONSISTENT MOVING AVG.

T1 = 9   T2 = 10   T3 = 11   T4 = 10   B1 = 8   B2 = 12   B3 = 10

B4 = 10

$$\text{Consistent Moving Average} = \frac{T1 + T2 + T3 + T4 + B1 + B2 + B3 + B4}{8}$$

$$= \frac{9 + 10 + 11 + 10 + 8 + 12 + 10 + 10}{8}$$

$$= 10$$

SYSTEM 12

OPTIMIZING YOUR MOVING AVERAGE

SYSTEM DEFINITIONS:

Suppose we are working with 19 day ESMA,

(1)   Put daily closing prices in Col. 1.

(2)   To start, add first 19 days, divide by 19 and put in Col. 2.

(3)   Smoothing constant for 19 day moving average is

$$\frac{2}{n+1} \ = \ \frac{2}{19+1} \ = \ \frac{2}{20} \ = \ .10$$

(4)   After a Buy signal is generated, assign Additional Smoothing Constant of .003 when a stock or commodity makes a new higher close. The new Cumulative Smoothing Constant (CSC) is calculated by adding daily Additional Smoothing Constant to the previous CSC until a maximum CSC of .13 is reached. Never go beyond 0.13. After sell signal return to CSC of 0.10. In the following example, the new higher closes are circled.

	Closing Price	Additonal Smoothing Constant	Cumulative Smoothing Constant (CSC)
Buy →	35.60	Start	.100
	(35.75)	.003	.103
	(36.00)	.003	.106
	(36.25)	.003	.109
	36.00	0	.109
	36.13	0	.109
	(36.50)	.003	.112
	(36.75)	.003	.115
	(37.00)	.003	.118
	36.50	0	.118

In Work Sheet, put Additional Smoothing Constant in Col. 3 and Cumulative Smoothing Constant (CSC) in Col. 4.

(5)   After a Sell signal is generated, assign Additional Smoothing Constant of .003 when a stock or commodity makes a new lower close. The new Cumulative Smoothing Constant (CSC) is calculated by adding daily Additional Smoothing Constant to the previous CSC until a maximum CSC of 0.13 is reached. Never go beyond 0.13. After Buy signal, return to CSC of 0.10. In the following example,   new lower closes are circled.

28

OPTIMIZING YOUR MOVING AVERAGE
Continued

Closing Price	Additional Smoothing Constant	Cumulative Smoothing Constant (CSC)
Sell ——➔ 36.00	Start	.100
(35.75)	.003	.103
(35.50)	.003	.106
35.63	0	.106
(35.25)	.003	.109
(35.00)	.003	.112
(34.50)	.003	.115
(34.25)	.003	.118
34.50	0	.118
(34.00)	.003	.121

(6)   New ESMA = Closing Price X CSC + Old ESMA (1- CSC)

Put New ESMA in Col. 5.

(7)   Col. 2 = Col. 5.

(8)   When a new Buy or Sell signal is generated, the old position is liquidated simultaneously. In other words, the system is always in the market.

DISCUSSION OF THE SYSTEM:

(1)   Research done by the author indicates that this is the best in moving averages.

(2)   During uptrend and downtrend, the system will give earlier Buy and Sell signals at important reversal points.

(3)   During Trading Range, your Cumulative Smoothing Constant (CSC) is almost the same as your regular Smoothing Constant.

(4)   This technique can be used with time and price filters as discussed before.

(5)   It is very simple and easy to calculate.

(6)   Does not require Top and Bottom to be well defined. Generation of Buy signal defines Bottom and vice versa.

(7)   Works very well for stocks as well as commodities.

WORK SHEET

SYSTEM 12

OPTIMIZING YOUR MOVING AVERAGE

		1 Daily Closing Price	2 19 Day Exponentially Smoothed Moving Average = Col. 5	3 Additional Smoothing Constant	4 Cumulative Smoothing Constant (CSC)	5 19 Day ESMA = Closing Price X Cumulative Smoothing Constant + ESMA (1- Cumulative Smoothing Constant)	
Buy	1	35.60	35.00	Start	.100		
	2	35.75	35.08	.003	.103	35.08	
	3	36.00	35.18	.003	.106	35.18	
	4	36.25	35.30	.003	.109	35.30	
	5	36.00	35.38	0	.109	35.38	
	6	36.13	35.46	0	.109	35.46	
	7	36.50	35.58	.003	.112	35.58	
	8	36.75	35.71	.003	.115	35.71	
	9	37.00	35.86	.003	.118	35.86	
	10	36.50	35.94	0	.118	35.94	
	11	37.25	36.10	.003	.121	36.10	
	12	37.50	36.27	.003	.124	36.27	
	13	37.25	36.39	0	.124	36.39	
	14	37.00	36.47	0	.124	36.47	
Sell	15	36.00	36.41	0	.124	36.41	Start with .10 again, after the Sell signal is generated.
	16						
Sell	17	36.00	36.41	Start	.100		
	18	35.75	36.34	.003	.103	36.34	
	19	35.50	36.25	.003	.106	36.25	
	20	35.63	36.18	0	.106	36.18	
	21	35.25	36.08	.003	.109	36.08	
	22	35.00	35.96	.003	.112	35.96	
	23	34.50	35.79	.003	.115	35.79	
	24	34.25	35.61	.003	.118	35.61	
	25	34.50	35.48	0	.118	35.48	
	26	34.50	35.36	0	.118	35.36	
	27	35.00	35.32	0	.118	35.32	
Buy	28	35.50	35.34	0	.118	35.34	Start with .10 again, after the Buy signal is generated.

SYSTEM 13

TWO MOVING AVERAGES

SYSTEM DEFINITIONS:

Suppose we are working with 7 day (faster) and 39 day (slower) moving averages, then

(1)   Put daily closing prices in Col. 1.

(2)   To start fast moving average, add seven closing prices, divide by seven and put in Col. 2.

(3)   Using a smoothing constant $\dfrac{2}{n+1} = \dfrac{2}{7+1} = \dfrac{2}{8} = .25,$

Find new ESMA = (closing price - old ESMA) x .25 + old ESMA.

Put this value in Col. 2.

(4)   To start slow moving average, add thirty-nine closing prices, divide by 39 and put in Col. 3.

(5)   Using a smoothing constant $\dfrac{2}{n+1} = \dfrac{2}{39+1} = \dfrac{2}{40} = .05,$

Find new ESMA = (closing price - old ESMA) x .05 + old ESMA.

Put this value in Col. 3.

(6)   Buy signal is generated when the faster (7 day) moving average crosses the slower (39 day) moving average on the upside.

(7)   Sell signal is generated when the faster (7 day) moving average crosses the slower (39 day) moving average on the downside.

(8)   When a new Buy or Sell signal is generated, the old position is liquidated simultaneously. In other words, the technique keeps you in the market all the time.

DISCUSSION OF THE SYSTEM:

(1)   Some moving average technicians believe that Buy and Sell signals based upon the crossings of faster and slower moving averages are effective and profitable. This is not always true. There are many whipsaws and losses based upon the cycles involved.

(2)   A single moving average with time and price filter is probably one of the best moving average systems.

WORK SHEET

SYSTEM 13

TWO MOVING AVERAGES

	1 Daily Closing Price	2 7 Day Exponentially Smoothed Moving Average of Col. 1	3 39 Day Exponentially Smoothed Moving Average of Col. 1	
1		36.50	37.50	
2	36.75	36.56	37.46	
3	37.00	36.67	37.44	
4	36.88	36.72	37.41	
5	37.00	36.79	37.39	
6	37.00	36.84	37.37	
7	37.25	36.95	37.37	
8	37.50	37.08	37.37	
9	37.75	37.25	37.39	
10	37.50	37.31	37.40	
11	(38.00)	(37.48)	(37.43)	→ Buy
12	37.25	37.43	37.42	
13	38.50	37.69	37.47	
14	39.00	38.02	37.55	
15	38.50	38.14	37.60	
16	38.25	38.17	37.63	
17	39.00	38.38	37.70	
18	38.00	38.28	37.71	
19	37.00	37.96	37.68	
20	37.50	37.85	37.67	
21	37.00	37.63	37.63	
22	(36.50)	(37.35)	(37.58)	→ Sell
23	36.00	37.01	37.50	
24	36.25	36.82	37.44	
25	35.75	36.55	37.35	
26	35.50	36.29	37.26	
27	35.25	36.03	37.16	

SYSTEM 13

TWO MOVING AVERAGES

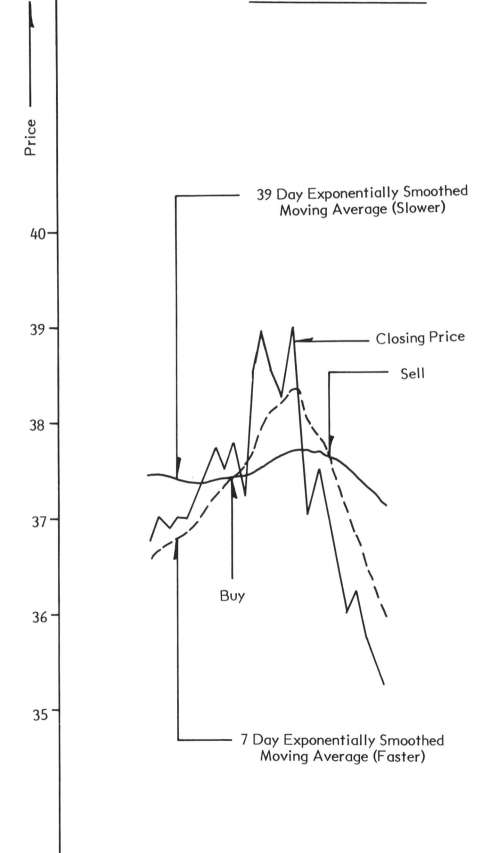

Price

39 Day Exponentially Smoothed
Moving Average (Slower)

Closing Price

Sell

Buy

7 Day Exponentially Smoothed
Moving Average (Faster)

33   Time

PRICE PROJECTION BASED ON MOVING AVERAGE

SYSTEM DEFINITIONS:

(1)   Put closing prices every other day in Col. 1, e.g., 35.00, 35.50, 36.00, 36.25, 36.50, 36.00, 36.75, 37.00, 36.50

(2)   We will be working with 20 day (fast) and 40 day (slow) moving averages. But since we are using alternate closing prices, we will be working with 10 unit and 20 unit moving averages. This will give the same results as daily closing prices but the labor involved in the calculations is reduced in half.

(3)   To start fast moving average, add first 10 closing prices recorded in Col. 1., divide by 10 and put in Col. 2.

(4)   Using a smoothing constant $\frac{2}{n+1}$ = $\frac{2}{10+1}$ = $\frac{2}{11}$ = 0.18,

Find new ESMA = (closing price - old ESMA) x .18 + old ESMA.

Put this value in Col. 2.

(5)   To start slow moving average, add first 20 closing prices, divide by 20 and put in Col. 3.

(6)   Using a smoothing constant $\frac{2}{n+1}$ = $\frac{2}{20+1}$ = $\frac{2}{21}$ = .10,

Find new ESMA = (closing prices - old ESMA) x .10 + old ESMA.

Put this value in Col. 3.

(7)   Plot 10 unit (or 20 day) moving average with 5 unit (or 10 day) lag.

(8)   Plot 20 unit (or 40 day) moving average with 10 unit (or 20 day) lag.

(9)   Identify the most recent top (T) of the stock or commodity.

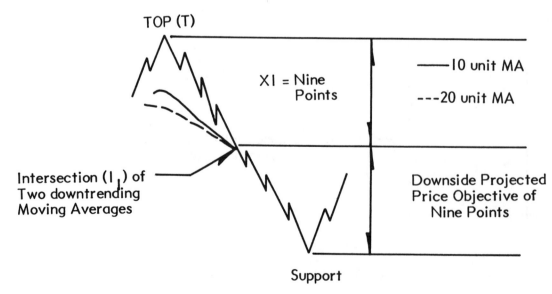

PRICE PROJECTION BASED ON MOVING AVERAGE
Continued

(10)   Also note the intersection (I_1) of the two downtrending (10 and 20 unit) moving averages.

(11)   Measure the vertical distance X_1 between the most recent top (T) and intersection (I_1) of the two moving averages.

(12)   Then the stock or commodity will usually travel the same distance X_1 before it finds support or a bottom.

(13)   Identify the most recent bottom (B) of the stock or commodity.

(14)   Also note the intersection (I_2) of the two uptrending (10 and 20 unit) moving averages.

(15)   Measure the vertical distance X_2 between the most recent bottom (B) and the intersection (I_2) of the two moving averages.

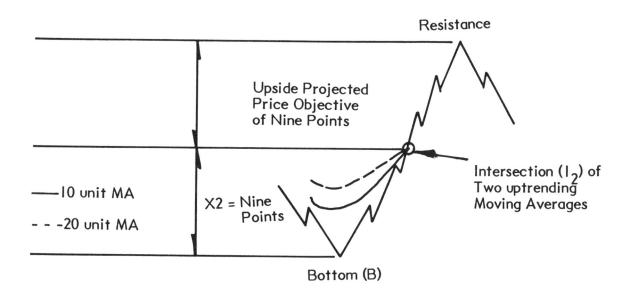

(16)   Then the stock or commodity will usually travel the same distance X_2 before it finds resistance or a top.

(17)   Repeat the same procedure.

WORK SHEET

SYSTEM 14

PRICE PROJECTION BASED ON MOVING AVERAGE

	1 Closing Price Every Other Day	2 10 Unit (or 20 Day) Exponentially Smoothed Moving Average of Col. 1	3 20 Unit (or 40 Day) Exponentially Smoothed Moving Average of Col. 1
1	36.50	35.90	36.23
2	36.25	35.96	36.20
3	36.88	36.13	36.30
4	35.75	36.06	36.24
5	35.25	35.91	36.14
6	35.13	35.77	36.04
7	35.00	35.63	35.94
8	34.50	35.43	35.79
9	35.38	35.42	35.75
10	36.75	35.66	35.85
11	36.13	35.74	35.88
12	35.88	35.77	35.88
13	36.00	35.81	35.89
14	37.13	36.05	36.02
15	36.88	36.20	36.10
16	37.13	36.37	36.20
17	36.38	36.37	36.22
18	34.75	36.08	36.08
19	34.25	35.75	35.89
20	35.00	35.61	35.80
21	34.63	35.44	35.69
22	34.25	35.22	35.54
23	34.50	35.09	35.44
24	33.63	34.83	35.27
25	33.50	34.59	35.09
26	33.50	34.39	34.92
27	34.88	34.48	34.92
28	35.00	34.57	34.93
29	34.25	34.52	34.86
30	34.13	34.45	34.79
31	35.88	34.70	34.90

PRICE PROJECTION BASED ON MOVING AVERAGE

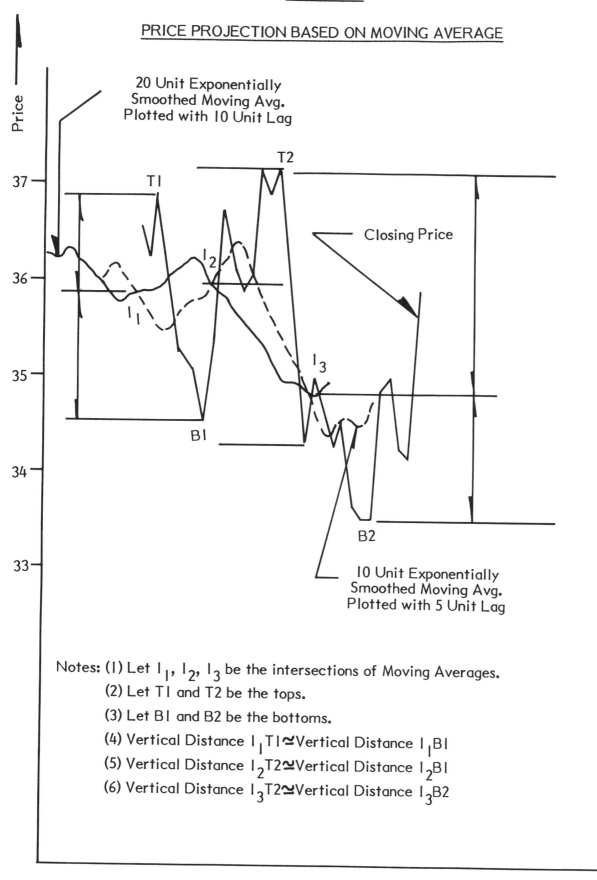

20 Unit Exponentially Smoothed Moving Avg. Plotted with 10 Unit Lag

T2

T1

Closing Price

I_2

I_1

I_3

B1

B2

10 Unit Exponentially Smoothed Moving Avg. Plotted with 5 Unit Lag

Notes: (1) Let I_1, I_2, I_3 be the intersections of Moving Averages.

     (2) Let T1 and T2 be the tops.

     (3) Let B1 and B2 be the bottoms.

     (4) Vertical Distance I_1T1 $\cong$ Vertical Distance I_1B1

     (5) Vertical Distance I_2T2 $\cong$ Vertical Distance I_2B1

     (6) Vertical Distance I_3T2 $\cong$ Vertical Distance I_3B2

Price

Time

SYSTEM 15

COMPOSITE MOVING AVERAGE

SYSTEM DEFINITIONS:

(1)   Col. 1 is the daily closing price.

(2)   Col. 2 is the 10 day exponentially smoothed moving average of Col. 1.

(3)   Col. 3 is the 20 day exponentially smoothed moving average of Col. 1.

(4)   Col. 4 is the 40 day exponentially smoothed moving average of Col. 1.

(5)   Col. 5 = Composite moving average = Col. 2 + Col. 3 + Col. 4 ÷ 3.

(6)   Buy signal is generated when the rising closing price penetrates the moving average on the upside.

(7)   Sell signal is generated when the falling closing price penetrates the moving average on the downside.

(8)   When a new Buy or Sell signal is generated, the old position is liquidated simultaneously. In other words, the system is always in the market.

DISCUSSION:

(1)   Since we are using the average of three different time cycles, the results are very good.

WORK SHEET

SYSTEM 15

COMPOSITE MOVING AVERAGE

	1 Daily Closing Price	2 10 Day Exponentially Smoothed Moving Average of Col. 1	3 20 Day Exponentially Smoothed Moving Average of Col. 1	4 40 Day Exponentially Smoothed Moving Average of Col. 1	5 = Col. 2 + Col. 3 + Col. 4 ÷ 3
1	45.60	46.50	46.72	46.95	46.72
2	45.00	46.23	46.55	46.85	46.54
3	44.00	45.83	46.29	46.71	46.28
4	43.75	45.45	46.04	46.56	46.02
5	44.25	45.24	45.86	46.45	45.85
6	44.75	45.15	45.75	46.36	45.75
7	45.00	45.12	45.67	46.29	45.70
8	(45.75)	45.24	45.68	46.27	(45.73) ←Buy
9	46.00	45.37	45.71	46.25	45.78
10	46.75	45.62	45.82	46.28	45.91
11	47.25	45.91	45.96	46.33	46.07
12	48.00	46.29	46.16	46.41	46.29
13	49.00	46.78	46.45	46.54	46.59
14	49.50	47.27	46.75	46.69	46.90
15	50.00	47.76	47.08	46.85	47.23
16	50.25	48.21	47.40	47.02	47.54
17	49.95	48.52	47.65	47.17	47.78
18	49.00	48.61	47.79	47.26	47.88
19	48.50	48.59	47.86	47.32	47.92
20	(47.00)	48.30	47.77	47.31	(47.79) ←Sell
21	46.00	47.89	47.59	47.24	47.57

SYSTEM 16

STEP WEIGHTED COMPOSITE MOVING AVERAGE

SYSTEM DEFINITIONS:

(1)   Col. 1 is the daily closing price.

(2)   Col. 2 is the 10 day exponentially smoothed moving average of Col. 1.

(3)   Col. 3 is the 20 day exponentially smoothed moving average of Col. 1.

(4)   Col. 4 is the 40 day exponentially smoothed moving average of Col. 1.

(5)   Col. 5 = Step Weighted Composite moving average = Col. 2 X .45 + Col. 3 X .35
       + Col. 4 X .20

(6)   Buy signal is generated when the rising closing price penetrates the moving
       average on the upside.

(7)   Sell signal is generated when the falling closing price penetrates the moving
       average on the downside.

(8)   When a new Buy or Sell signal is generated, the old position is liquidated simul-
       taneously. In other words, the system is always in the market.

DISCUSSION:

(1)   Since we are using Step Weighted Composite moving average, we will get
       earlier Buy and Sell signals at important reversal points.

WORK SHEET

SYSTEM 16

STEP WEIGHTED COMPOSITE MOVING AVERAGE

	1 Daily Closing Price	2 10 Day Exponentially Smoothed Moving Average of Col. 1	3 20 Day Exponentially Smoothed Moving Average of Col. 1	4 40 Day Exponentially Smoothed Moving Average of Col. 1	5 = Col. 2 x .45 + Col. 3 x .35 + Col. 4 x .20
1	45.60	46.50	46.72	46.95	46.67
2	45.00	46.23	46.55	46.85	46.47
3	44.00	45.83	46.29	46.71	46.17
4	43.75	45.45	46.04	46.56	45.88
5	44.25	45.24	45.86	46.45	45.70
6	44.75	45.15	45.75	46.36	45.60
7	45.00	45.12	45.67	46.29	45.55
8	(45.75)	45.24	45.68	46.27	(45.60) ⟵ Buy
9	46.00	45.37	45.71	46.25	45.67
10	46.75	45.62	45.82	46.28	45.82
11	47.25	45.91	45.96	46.33	46.01
12	48.00	46.29	46.16	46.41	46.27
13	49.00	46.78	46.45	46.54	46.61
14	49.50	47.27	46.75	46.69	46.97
15	50.00	47.76	47.08	46.85	47.34
16	50.25	48.21	47.40	47.02	47.69
17	49.95	48.52	47.65	47.17	47.95
18	49.00	48.61	47.79	47.26	48.05
19	48.50	48.59	47.86	47.32	48.08
20	(47.00)	48.30	47.77	47.31	(47.92) ⟵ Sell
21	46.00	47.89	47.59	47.24	47.66
22	46.50	47.64	47.49	47.20	47.50
23	46.20	47.38	47.36	47.15	47.33
24	46.75	47.27	47.30	47.13	47.25
25	46.50	47.13	47.22	47.10	47.16

SYSTEM 17

MOVING AVERAGE SYSTEMS

GENERAL DISCUSSION:

(1)   Trend lines which are fitted by inspection, by drawing them across two or more successive tops or bottoms, involve elements of judgement first in projecting and later in adjusting them after a trend has accelerated.

(2)   Moving average computed mathematically does not require any element of judgement and can be used as a mechanical method.

(3)   Moving average is a trend-following technique that does not do any predicting.

(4)   Moving average emphasizes the direction of trend, provides a means of confirming a trend reversal and smooths out numerous meaningless fluctuations.

(5)   The moving average with more days or data is more smooth (or slow) with longer lag to latest price.

(6)   The moving average with fewer days or data is less smooth (or fast) with shorter lag to latest price.

(7)   The moving average can be plotted coincident with latest closing price.

(8)   The moving average can be plotted with a lead to latest price. This advances the moving average without changing the slope of the line to get earlier signals with minimum whipsaws during the trading range.

(9)   The moving average can also be plotted with a lag to latest price. The lag waits until the new trend is well defined to get earlier signals with minimum whipsaws during the trading range. This technique is very useful for future price projection already discussed in System 14.

(10)   Lead and lag techniques can use the same Buy and Sell signals as coincident average.

(11)   Moving average can be constructed from (a) closing price, (b) Average of High & Low price and (c) Average of High, Low and close price.

(12)   In trading range, moving average is almost a useless working tool. Unless these characteristics are very well understood, it is a dangerous tool and likely to be very costly to stock/commodity traders.

(13)   During an uptrend the prices determining the moving average are generally smaller than the current price, hence the current price tends to stay above the moving average.

(14)   During a downtrend, the prices determining the moving average are generally larger than the current price, hence the current price tends to stay below the moving average.

(15)   In a trading range, the price determining the moving average is almost the same as the current price and hence the current price randomly fluctuates around the moving average giving false Buy and Sell signals.

MOVING AVERAGE SYSTEM
Continued

(16)   If the period of moving average is shortened, the moving average gives more Buy and Sell signals, thereby increasing trading losses and brokerage commissions but furnishing earlier signals at important reversal points.

(17)   If the period of moving average is lengthened, the moving average gives fewer Buy and Sell signals, thereby eliminating many losses that result from false penetrations, but delaying signals at reversal points with consequent loss of potential profits.

(18)   Moving average is the most widely used and least understood method for trading.

(19)   Moving average is a very useful tool if you know when and how to use it.

SYSTEM 18

PRACTICAL APPLICATIONS OF MOVING AVERAGES

GENERAL DISCUSSION:

(1)   N day moving average can be calculated by adding two $\frac{N}{2}$ day moving averages $\frac{N}{2}$ days apart and dividing by Two. e.g. Let N = 20. Then 20 day moving average can be calculated by adding two 10 day moving averages 10 days apart and dividing by two.

(2)   N day moving average can be calculated by adding three $\frac{N}{3}$ day moving averages each $\frac{N}{3}$ days apart and dividing by Three. e.g. Let N = 30. Then 30 day moving average can be calculated by adding three 10 day moving averages each 10 days apart and dividing by Three.

(3)   N day moving average can be calculated by adding four $\frac{N}{4}$ day moving averages each $\frac{N}{4}$ days apart and dividing by four. e.g. Let N = 40. Then 40 day moving average can be calculated by adding four 10 day moving averages each 10 days apart and dividing by four.

(4)   Initially when you start working on any stock or commodity, use weekly data instead of daily data for the first initial reading of moving average. e.g. 8 week moving average instead of 40 day moving average.

(5)   Extensive research done by some commodity brokerage houses and advisory services suggests the following optimum length for general guide lines.

        (A)   Single Moving Average

Commodity	Days
Cocoa	55
Corn	50
Sugar	64
Cotton	65
Silver	30
Copper	68
Soybeans	55
Soybean Meal	55
Wheat	50
Pork Bellies	22
Soybean Oil	55
Plywood	65
Live Hogs	25
Live Cattle	33

PRACTICAL APPLICATIONS OF MOVING AVERAGES
Continued

(B) Two Moving Averages

Commodity	Days
Cocoa	7, 25
Corn	11, 47
Sugar	5, 50
Cotton	16, 25
Silver	4, 26
Copper	17, 33
Soybeans	16, 50
Soybean Meal	18, 50
Wheat	11, 47
Pork Bellies	25, 46
Soybean Oil	14, 50
Plywood	24, 42
Live Hogs	3, 14
Live Cattle	7, 13
Ginnie Maes	4, 36
T-Bills	6, 18
Gold	14, 50

(6)   Scalpers and short term stock/option traders:

20 Hour moving average for stocks with high volatility.

30 Hour moving average for stocks with medium volatility.

40 Hour moving average for stocks with low volatility.

(7)   Intermediate Term stock/option traders:

20 Day moving average for stocks with high volatility.

30 Day moving average for stocks with medium volatility.

40 Day moving average for stocks with low volatility.

(8)   Long Term stock/option traders:

150 Day moving average for stocks with high volatility.

175 Day moving average for stocks with medium volatility.

200 Day moving average for stocks with low volatility.

PRACTICAL APPLICATIONS OF MOVING AVERAGES
Continued

(9)   Single moving average without any filter (Time or Price) is a very inadequate technical tool likely to be too costly to stock/commodity traders.

(10)   Single moving average with time filter is a good technical tool.

(11)   Single moving average with time and price filter is a better technical tool.

(12)   Optimized single moving average with time and price filter is the best technical tool.

SYSTEM 19

JOSEPH GRANVILLE'S ON BALANCE VOLUME

GENERAL THEORY & DISCUSSION:

(1)   Was developed by Joseph Granville.

(2)   Determines Accumulation/Distribution by volume.

(3)   Based on the assumption that volume trends lead price trends.

(4)   When the closing price for the day (or week) is up, the total volume for that day (or week) is considered positive or Buy volume.

(5)   When the closing price for the day (or week) is down, the total volume for that day (or week) is considered negative or Sell volume.

(6)   The cumulative On Balance Volume (OBV) is calculated by adding or subtracting daily or weekly volume, depending on whether it is Buy or Sell volume.

(7)   If the cumulative OBV is positive, the stock is under accumulation and vice versa.

(8)   Accumulated volume line is plotted under the price line.

(9)   OBV is interpreted in the same way as price charts.

(10)   Higher highs and higher lows is bullish.

(11)   Lower highs and lower lows is bearish.

(12)   Peaks and troughs in OBV indicate trend reversals.

(13)   Divergence between OBV and price is the most important Buy or Sell signal you can get from OBV.

(14)   Rising stock prices with flat or falling OBV suggest weakness. Thus, a trend reversal to the downside can take place.

(15)   Falling stock prices with flat or rising OBV suggest strength. A trend reversal to the upside can take place.

(16)   If OBV breaks out on the upside, the stock prices should follow the same trend.

(17)   If OBV breaks out on the downside, the stock prices should follow the same trend.

JOSEPH GRANVILLE'S ON BALANCE VOLUME
Continued

(18)   Compare OBV levels for the same price levels. e.g.

36.50	-5000		37.50	5000
		Suggests		Suggests
		Strength		Weakness
36.50	4000		37.00	1000

(19)   Works well during price breakouts after Accumulation/Distribution.

(20)   Based on this author's experience, OBV works well with weekly prices instead of daily prices because we are using the benefit of a time filter.

(21)   You can try OBV on a daily or weekly basis depending on your choice.

(22)   Interpretation of OBV is very simple in theory but extremely complex in reality when you compare the universe of some 5000 to 6000 stocks.

(23)   Inter-day (or Inter-week) method.

(24)   Author has developed a completely mechanical method of trading that does not require human judgement.

SYSTEM DEFINITIONS: (Method A)

(1)   Col. 1 is the weekly closing price.

(2)   Col. 2 is positive if the price (compared to previous price) is up and vice versa.

(3)   Col. 3 is the weekly volume.

(4)   Col. 4 is Buy or positive volume if Col. 2 is positive. Col. 4 is Sell or negative volume if Col. 2 is negative.

(5)   Col. 5 is the cumulative On Balance Volume (OBV) calculated by adding or subtracting volumes in Col. 4.

(6)   Col. 6 is the 10 week exponentially smoothed moving average of Col. 5.

(7)   Buy signal is generated when the bottom reversal point in Col. 6 exceeds by 6%.

(8)   Sell signal is generated when the top reversal point in Col. 6 declines by 6%.

(9)   When a new Buy or Sell signal is generated, the old position is liquidated simultaneously. In other words, the system keeps you in the market all the time.

SYSTEM 19

JOSEPH GRANVILLE'S ON BALANCE VOLUME
Continued

SYSTEM DEFINITIONS: (Method B)

(1)   Col. I is the weekly closing price.

(2)   Col. 2 is positive if the price (compared to previous price) is up and vice versa.

(3)   Col. 3 is the weekly volume.

(4)   Col. 4 is the Buy or positive volume if Col. 2 is positive.

(5)   Col. 5 is the Sell or negative volume if Col. 2 is negative.

(6)   Col. 6 is the 10 week exponentially smoothed moving average of Col. 4.

(7)   Col. 7 is the 10 week exponentially smoothed moving average of Col. 5.

(8)   Buy signal is generated when the positive volume (Col. 6) crosses negative volume (Col. 7) on the upside by 6%.

(9)   Sell signal is generated when the positive volume (Col. 6) crosses negative volume (Col. 7) on the downside by 6%.

(10)   When a new Buy or Sell signal is generated, the old position is liquidated simultaneously. In other words, the system keeps you in the market all the time.

WORK SHEET

SYSTEM 19 (Method A)

JOSEPH GRANVILLE'S ON BALANCE VOLUME

	1 Weekly Closing Price	2 + or – Compared to Previous Price	3 Weekly Volume	4 Buy or Sell Volume	5 Cumulative On Balance Volume	6 10 Week Exponentially Smoothed Moving Average of Col. 5	
1	46.00						
2	46.25	+	520	+520	520		
3	46.00	–	430	–430	90		
4	45.75	–	880	–880	–790		
5	45.50	–	660	–660	–1450		
6	45.25	–	750	–750	–2200		
7	47.25	+	990	+990	–1210		
8	48.75	+	1075	+1075	–135		
9	50.63	+	1073	+1073	938		
10	52.88	+	1324	+1324	2262		
11	52.25	–	1275	–1275	987	–988	
12	54.50	+	1390	+1390	2377	–382	
13	54.75	+	1890	+1890	4267	455	
14	55.38	+	1075	+1075	5342	1334	
15	56.50	+	672	+672	6014	2177	
16	60.63	+	1450	+1450	7464	3128	
17	58.50	–	970	–970	6494	3734	
18	57.25	–	735	–735	5759	4099	
19	56.13	–	530	–530	5229	4302	
20	55.00	–	625	–625	4604	4356	Top
21	54.50	–	720	–720	3884	4271	
22	53.25	–	540	–540	3344	4104	
23	(53.50)	+	520	+520	3864	(4061)	Sell
24	53.25	–	770	–770	3094	3887	
25	54.00	+	640	+640	3734	3860	Bottom
26	54.25	+	920	+920	4654	4003	
27	(55.00)	+	780	+780	5434	(4260)	Buy
28	54.25	–	845	–845	4589	4319	
29	56.00	+	990	+990	5579	4546	
30	57.00	+	1050	+1050	6629	4921	
31	58.50	+	1200	+1200	7829	5444	

WORK SHEET

SYSTEM 19 (Method B)

JOSEPH GRANVILLE'S ON BALANCE VOLUME

	1 Weekly Closing Price	2 + or - Compared to Previous Price	3 Weekly Volume	4 Buy or Positive Volume	5 Sell or Negative Volume	6 10 Week Exponentially Smoothed Moving Average of Col. 4	6 10 Week Exponentially Smoothed Moving Average of Col. 5	
1	45.75							
2	45.50	−	477	0	477			
3	45.75	+	275	275	0			
4	46.00	+	360	360	0			
5	46.25	+	520	520	0			
6	46.00	−	430	0	430			
7	45.75	−	880	0	880			
8	45.50	−	660	0	660			
9	45.25	−	750	0	750			
10	47.25	+	990	990	0			
11	48.75	+	1075	1075	0	322	320	
12	(50.63)	+	1073	1073	0	(457)	(262)	Buy
13	52.88	+	1324	1324	0	613	215	
14	52.25	−	1275	0	1275	503	406	
15	54.50	+	1390	1390	0	663	333	
16	54.75	+	1890	1890	0	883	273	
17	55.38	+	1075	1075	0	918	224	
18	56.50	+	672	672	0	874	183	
19	60.63	+	1450	1450	0	977	150	
20	58.50	−	970	0	970	801	298	
21	57.25	−	735	0	735	657	377	
22	56.13	−	530	0	530	539	404	
23	55.00	−	625	0	625	442	444	
24	(54.50)	−	720	0	720	(362)	(494)	Sell
25	53.25	−	540	0	540	297	502	
26	53.50	+	520	520	0	337	412	
27	53.25	−	770	0	770	277	476	
28	54.00	+	640	640	0	342	390	
29	(54.25)	+	920	920	0	(446)	(320)	Buy
30	55.00	+	780	780	0	506	263	
31	54.25	−	845	845	845	415	367	

SYSTEM 20

NEGATIVE ON BALANCE VOLUME

GENERAL THEORY & DISCUSSION:

(1)   Determines supply/demand by price change on declining volume days (or weeks).

(2)   Look only at the day (or week) when the volume has declined from the previous day (or week).

(3)   If the volume for the day (or week) has increased from the previous day (or week), the volume is assigned no or zero value.

(4)   If the price is up on a declining volume day, the volume for that day is positive.

(5)   If the price is down on a declining volume day, the volume for that day is negative.

(6)   The cumulative Negative On Balance Volume is calculated by adding daily volumes (positive, negative or zero).

(7)   Flat Negative On Balance Volume trend is neutral or mildly bullish.

(8)   Upward sloping Negative On Balance Volume trend is bullish.

(9)   Downward sloping Negative On Balance Volume trend is bearish.

(10)   Since majority of stocks have an overall trend of price declines on lower volumes, this is a very useful technical tool.

(11)   Inter-day (or Inter-week) method.

SYSTEM DEFINITIONS: (Method A)

(1)   Col. 1 is the weekly closing price.

(2)   Col. 2 is the weekly volume.

(3)   If the price is up on a declining volume week, assign positive (+) to volume.

   If the price is down on a declining volume week, assign negative (-) to volume.

   If there is no change in price on a declining week, assign zero.

   Put the above values in Col. 3.

(4)   Col. 4 is the cumulative Negative On Balance Volume calculated by adding or subtracting volumes in Col. 3.

(5)   See work sheet for the explanation of Buy and Sell signals.

52

SYSTEM 20

NEGATIVE ON BALANCE VOLUME
Continued

SYSTEM DEFINITIONS: (Method B)

(1)   Col. 1 is the weekly closing price.

(2)   Col. 2 is the weekly volume.

(3)   If the price is up on a declining volume week, assign positive (+) to volume.

If the price is down on a declining volume week, assign negative (-) to volume.

If there is no change in price on a declining volume week assign zero.

Put the above values in Col. 3.

(4)   Col. 4 is the positive volume.

(5)   Col. 5 is the negative volume.

(6)   Col. 6 is the 10 week exponentially smoothed moving average of Col. 4.

(7)   Col. 7 is the 10 week exponentially smoothed moving average of Col. 5.

(8)   Col. 8   = Col. 6   - Col. 7.

(9)   Col. 9 is the Accumulation of Col. 8.

(10)   Buy signal is generated when the bottom reversal point in Col. 9 exceeds by 6%.

(11)   Sell signal is generated when the top reversal point in Col. 9 declines by 6%.

(12)   When a new Buy or Sell signal is generated, the old position is liquidated simultaneously. In other words, the system keeps you in the market all the time.

WORK SHEET

SYSTEM 20 (Method A)

NEGATIVE ON BALANCE VOLUME

	1 Weekly Closing Price	2 Weekly Volume	3 Volume Based on Price Change	4 Accumulation of Col. 3	
1	31.00	206			
2	30.50	178	-178	-178	
3	30.75	200	0	-178	
4	30.50	171	-171	-349	
5	31.00	400	0	-349	Downward sloping Negative On Balance Volume is Bearish.
6	30.50	300	-300	-649	
7	30.00	210	-210	-859	
8	29.50	175	-175	-1034	
9	29.75	215	0	-1034	
10	29.50	207	-207	-1241	
11	28.50	195	-195	-1436	
12	28.00	160	-160	-1596	
13	27.00	140	-140	-1736	
14	27.50	160	0	-1736	
15	27.75	175	0	-1736	Flat Negative On Balance Volume is Neutral or mildly Bullish.
16	28.00	210	0	-1736	
17	28.25	300	0	-1736	
18	28.50	277	+277	-1459	
19	28.75	175	+175	-1284	
20	29.00	325	0	-1284	
21	29.50	275	+275	-1009	
22	30.00	250	+250	-759	
23	29.50	425	0	-759	Upward sloping Negative On Balance Volume is Bullish.
24	30.00	389	+389	-370	
25	30.50	350	+350	-20	
26	31.00	303	+303	+283	

SYSTEM 20 (Method B)

NEGATIVE ON BALANCE VOLUME

	1 Weekly Closing Price	2 Weekly Volume	3 Volume Based on Price Change	4 Positive Volume	5 Negative Volume	6 10 Week ESMA of Col. 4	7 10 Week ESMA of Col. 5	8 = Col. 6 − Col. 7	9 Accumulation of Col. 8	
1	31.00	206								
2	30.50	178	−178	0	178					
3	30.75	200	0	0	0					
4	30.50	171	−171	0	171					
5	31.00	400	0	0	0					
6	30.50	300	−300	0	300					
7	30.00	210	−210	0	210					
8	29.50	175	−175	0	175					
9	29.75	215	0	0	0					
10	29.50	207	−207	0	207					
11	28.50	195	−195	0	195	0	144	−144	−144	
12	28.00	160	−160	0	160	0	147	−147	−291	
13	27.00	140	−140	0	140	0	145	−145	−436	
14	27.50	160	0	0	0	0	119	−119	−555	
15	27.75	175	0	0	0	0	98	−98	−653	
16	28.00	210	0	0	0	0	80	−80	−733	
17	28.25	300	0	0	0	0	66	−66	−799	
18	28.50	277	+277	277	0	50	54	−4	−803	Bottom
19	28.75	175	+175	175	0	72	44	27	−776	
20	29.00	325	0	0	0	59	36	23	−753	Buy
21	29.50	275	+275	275	0	98	30	68	−685	
22	30.00	250	+250	250	0	125	24	101	−584	
23	29.50	425	0	0	0	103	19	84	−500	
24	30.00	389	+389	389	0	154	16	138	−362	
25	30.50	350	+350	350	0	190	13	177	−185	
26	31.00	303	+303	303	0	210	11	199	14	

SYSTEM 21

VOLUME PRICE TREND ANALYSIS

GENERAL THEORY AND DISCUSSION:

(1)   Developed by David Markstein.

(2)   Determines Accumulation/Distribution by volume and price change.

(3)   When the closing price for the day (or week) is up, the total volume for that day (or week) is multiplied by positive change in price to get positive Flow of Money.

(4)   When the closing for the day (or week) is down, the total volume for that day (or week) is multiplied by negative change in price to get negative Flow of Money.

(5)   The cumulative Flow of Money is calculated by adding daily (or weekly) values.

(6)   If the cumulative Flow of Money is positive, then the stock is under accumulation.

(7)   If the cumulative Flow of Money is negative, then the stock is under distribution.

(8)   Accumulated Flow of Money line is plotted under the price line.

(9)   Interpretation of the results is the same as Joseph Granville's On Balance volume, system 19.

(10)   Inter-day (or Inter-week) method.

SYSTEM DEFINITIONS: (METHOD A)

(1)   Col. 1 is the weekly closing price.

(2)   Col. 2 is the change in price compared to previous price.

(3)   Col. 3 is the weekly volume.

(4)   Col. 4 = Col. 2 x Col. 3.

(5)   Col. 5 is the accumulation of Col. 4.

(6)   Col. 6 is the 10 week exponentially smoothed moving average of Col. 5.

(7)   Buy signal is generated, when the bottom reversal point in Col. 6 exceeds by 6%.

(8)   Sell Signal is generated, when the top reversal point in Col. 6 declines by 6%.

(9)   When a new Buy or Sell signal is generated, the old position is liquidated simultaneously. In other words, the system is always in the market.

SYSTEM DEFINITIONS: (METHOD B)

(1)   Col. 1 is the closing price.

(2)   Col. 2 is the change in price compared to previous price.

(3)   Col. 3 is the weekly volume.

(4)   Col. 4 = Col. 2 x Col. 3, if Col. 2 is positive.

(5)   Col. 5 = Col. 2 x Col. 3, if Col. 2 is negative.

(6)   Col. 6 is the 10 week exponentially smoothed moving average of Col. 4.

(7)   Col. 7 is the 10 week exponentially smoothed moving average of Col. 5.

(8)   Buy signal is generated, when positive money flow (Col. 6) crosses negative money flow (Col. 7) on the upside by 6%.

(9)   Sell signal is generated, when positive money flow (Col. 6) crosses negative money flow (Col. 7) on the downside by 6%.

(10)   When a new Buy or Sell signal is generated, the old position is liquidated simultaneously. In other words, the system is always in the market.

WORK SHEET

SYSTEM 21 (Method A)

VOLUME PRICE TREND ANALYSIS

	1 Weekly Closing Price	2 Change in Price vs. Previous Price	3 Weekly Volume	4 = Col. 2 x Col. 3	5 Accumulation of Col. 4	6 10 Week Exponentially Smoothed Moving Average of Col. 5
1	46.00					
2	46.25	+.25	520	+130	130	
3	46.00	-.25	430	-107	23	
4	45.75	-.25	880	-220	-197	
5	45.50	-.25	660	-165	-362	
6	45.25	-.25	750	-187	-549	
7	47.25	+2.00	990	+1980	1431	
8	48.75	+1.50	1075	+1613	3043	
9	50.63	+1.88	1073	+2017	5060	
10	52.88	+2.25	1324	+2979	8039	
11	52.25	-.63	1275	-803	7236	2385
12	54.50	+2.25	1390	+3127	10363	3821
13	54.75	+.25	1890	+472	10835	5084
14	55.38	+.63	1075	+677	11512	6241
15	56.50	+1.12	672	+753	12265	7325
16	60.63	+4.13	1450	+5988	18253	9292
17	58.50	-2.13	970	-2066	16187	10533
18	57.25	-1.25	735	-919	15268	11386
19	56.13	-1.12	530	-594	14674	11977
20	55.00	-1.13	625	-706	13968	12335
21	54.50	-.50	720	-360	13608	12565
22	53.25	-1.25	540	-675	12933	12631
23	53.50	+.25	520	+130	13063	12709
24	53.25	-.25	770	-193	12870	12738
25	54.00	+.75	640	+480	13350	12848
26	54.25	+.25	920	+230	13580	12980
27	55.00	+.75	780	+585	14165	13193
28	54.25	-.75	845	-634	13531	13254
29	56.00	+1.75	990	+1733	15264	13616
30	57.00	+1.00	1050	+1050	16314	14101

WORK SHEET

SYSTEM 21 (Method B)

VOLUME PRICE TREND ANALYSIS

	1 Weekly Closing Price	2 Change in Price vs. Previous Price	3 Weekly Volume	4 = Col. 2 X Col. 3 with Positive Sign	5 = Col. 2 X Col. 3 with Negative Sign	6 10 Week Exponentially Smoothed Moving Average of Col. 4	7 10 Week Exponentially Smoothed Moving Average of Col. 5
1	46.00						
2	46.25	+.25	520	130	0		
3	46.00	-.25	430	0	107		
4	45.75	-.25	880	0	220		
5	45.50	-.25	660	0	165		
6	45.25	-.25	750	0	187		
7	47.25	+2.00	990	1980	0		
8	48.75	+1.50	1075	1612	0		
9	50.63	+1.88	1073	2017	0		
10	52.88	+2.25	1324	2979	0		
11	52.25	-.63	1275	0	803	872	148
12	54.50	+2.25	1390	3127	0	1275	122
13	54.75	+.25	1890	472	0	1133	100
14	55.38	+.63	1075	677	0	1051	82
15	56.50	+1.12	672	753	0	997	67
16	60.63	+4.13	1450	5988	0	1895	55
17	58.50	-2.13	970	0	2066	1554	417
18	57.25	-1.25	735	0	919	1275	507
19	56.13	-1.12	530	0	594	1045	523
20	55.00	-1.13	625	0	706	857	556
21	54.50	-.50	720	0	360	703	521
22	53.25	-1.25	540	0	675	576	548
23	53.50	+.25	520	130	0	496	450
24	53.25	-.25	770	0	193	407	403
25	54.00	+.75	640	480	0	420	331
26	54.25	+.25	920	230	0	386	271
27	55.00	+.75	780	585	0	422	222
28	54.25	-.75	845	0	634	346	297
29	56.00	+1.75	990	1733	0	595	243
30	57.00	+1.00	1050	1050	0	677	199
31	58.50	+1.50	1200	1800	0	879	164

SYSTEM 22

DON WORDEN'S TICK VOLUME

GENERAL THEORY AND DISCUSSION:

(1)   Developed by Don Worden.

(2)   Fundamental difference between this technique and other techniques (OBV, Negative On Balance volume, and Price Volume Trend)is that tick volume takes into consideration intra-day volume whereas others take into consideration only inter-day volume.

(3)   Refined method of measuring Accumulation/Distribution using daily stock trading transactions on a trade by trade basis.

(4)   Compare the price with previous trade. If there is no change in price, put the volume in no tick volume column.

(5)   Compare the price with previous trade. If there is a positive change in price, put the volume in up tick volume column.

(6)   Compare the price with previous trade. If there is a negative change in price, put the volume in down tick volume column.

(7)   At the end of the day, add volumes in up tick, down tick and no tick columns.

(8)   If the up tick volume is greater than the down tick volume (neglecting no tick volume), Accumulation or Buying is taking place in the market. The differential is positive (up tick transactions).

(9)   If the down tick volume is greater than the up tick volume (neglecting no tick volume), Distribution or selling is taking place in the market. The differential is negative (down tick transactions).

(10)   The cumulative On Balance volume is calculated by adding daily positive or negative differentials.

(11)   If the cumulative OBV is positive, the stock is under accumulation.

(12)   If the cumulative OBV is negative, the stock is under distribution.

(13)   Accumulated volume line is plotted under the price line.

(14)   10, 30, and 60 day moving totals of the cumulative volume is plotted.

(15)   Buy signal is generated when the stock shows consistent Buying Pressure (Positive differentials or up tick transactions).

(16)   Sell signal is generated when the stock shows consistent selling pressure (negative differentials or down tick transactions).

(17)   There is no practical way for average Trader/Investor to get his own data.

WORK SHEET

SYSTEM 22

DON WORDEN'S TICK VOLUME

	1	2	3	4	5
	Volume on a trade by trade basis	Price during a given trade	Up tick volume	Down tick volume	No tick volume
1	100	34			
2	200	34	0	0	200
3	300	34 1/8	300	0	0
4	100	34 1/8	0	0	100
5	200	34 1/8	0	0	200
6	100	34	0	100	0
7	400	33 3/4	0	400	0
8	500	33 3/4	0	0	500
9	1000	33 1/2	0	1000	0
10	100	33 1/2	0	0	100
11	500	33 1/4	0	500	0
12	200	33 1/4	0	0	200
13	300	33	0	300	0
14	600	33 1/8	600	0	0
15	200	33	0	200	0
16	100	33	0	0	100
17	100	33	0	0	100
TOTAL			900	2500	1500

SYSTEM 23

LARRY WILLIAMS' ACCUMULATION/DISTRIBUTION METHOD

GENERAL THEORY AND DISCUSSION:

(1)   Developed by Larry Williams.

(2)   Determines Accumulation/Distribution by volume and price change.

(3)   Intra-day or Intra-week method.

(4)   Net Buying or selling pressure = $\left(\dfrac{C-O}{H-L}\right)$ V. Where

O = Open   C = Close   H = High   L = Low   V = Volume

(5)   When the opening price is less than the closing price, there is net buying.

(6)   When the opening price is greater than the closing price, there is net selling.

(7)   The cumulative Flow of Money is calculated by adding daily (or weekly) Buying or selling pressure.

(8)   If the cumulative Flow of Money is positive, then the stock is under accumulation.

(9)   If the cumulative Flow of Money is negative, then the stock is under distribution.

(10)   Accumulated Flow of Money line is plotted under the price line.

(11)   Interpretation of the results is the same as Joseph Granville's On Balance volume, system 19.

(12)   One of the biggest disadvantages of this system is that 'Patterson News', Patterson, New Jersey, is the only newspaper that publishes open, high, low and close for New York stock exchange stocks only.

(13)   On weekly basis, Barron's publishes only high, low and close for all stocks on all exchanges.

(14)   Closing price of the previous day or week can be used as opening price for today or this week.

SYSTEM DEFINITIONS: (METHOD A)

(1)   Col. 1 is the weekly opening price. Previous week's closing price is used as opening price.

(2)   Col. 2 is the weekly high price.

(3)   Col. 3 is the weekly low price.

SYSTEM 23 (Con't)

(4)   Col. 4 is the weekly close price.

(5)   Col. 5 is the weekly volume.

(6)   Col. 6 is calculated using formula $= \left(\dfrac{C-O}{H-L} \right) V$

(7)   Col. 7 is the accumulation of Col. 6.

(8)   Col. 8 is the 10 week exponentially smoothed moving average of Col. 7.

(9)   Buy signal is generated, when the bottom reversal point in Col. 8 exceeds by 6%.

(10)   Sell signal is generated, when the top reversal point in Col. 8 declines by 6%.

(11)   When a new Buy or Sell signal is generated, the old position is liquidated simultaneously. In other words, the system keeps you in the market all the time.

SYSTEM DEFINITIONS: (METHOD B)

(1)   Col. 1 is the weekly opening price. Previous week's closing price is used as opening price.

(2)   Col. 2 is the weekly high price.

(3)   Col. 3 is the weekly low price.

(4)   Col. 4 is the weekly close price.

(5)   Col. 5 is the weekly volume.

(6)   Col. 6 is positive money flow, when O is less than C.

(7)   Col. 7 is negative money flow, when C is less than O.

(8)   Col. 8 is the 10 week exponentially smoothed moving average of Col. 6.

(9)   Col. 9 is the 10 week exponentially smoothed moving average of Col. 7.

(10)   Buy signal is generated when the positive money flow (Col. 8) crosses negative money flow (Col. 9) on the upside by 6%.

(11)   Sell signal is generated when the positive money flow (Col. 8) crosses negative money flow (Col. 9) on the downside by 6%.

(12)   When a new Buy or Sell signal is generated, the old position is liquidated simultaneously. In other words, the system is always in the market.

SPECIAL NOTE: Since we are using previous day or previous week's closing price as opening price, this technique is an inter-day or inter-week method instead of intra-day or intra-week method.

WORK SHEET

SYSTEM 23 (Method A)

LARRY WILLIAMS' ACCUMULATION/DISTRIBUTION METHOD

	1 Weekly Open Price	2 Weekly High Price	3 Weekly Low Price	4 Weekly Close Price	5 Weekly Volume	6 = $\frac{4-1}{2-3} \times 5$	7 Accumulation of Col. 6	8 10 Week Exponentially Smoothed Moving Average of Col. 7	
1	47.75	48.88	46.50	46.88	3085	-1128	-1128		
2	46.88	47.38	45.63	46.25	2825	-1017	-2145		
3	46.25	49.00	45.63	49.00	3778	3083	938		
4	49.00	50.75	48.75	49.75	4936	1851	2789		
5	49.75	50.13	47.00	47.13	2711	-2269	520		
6	47.13	48.50	46.88	48.13	3075	1898	2418		
7	48.13	48.63	47.25	48.25	1955	170	2588		
8	48.25	48.50	46.50	47.75	2021	-505	2083		
9	47.75	49.75	47.50	49.50	2011	1564	3647		
10	49.50	50.25	49.25	49.50	8495	0	3647	1536	
11	49.50	51.38	49.25	51.38	4862	4291	7938	2688	
12	51.38	55.00	51.00	54.75	5351	4508	12446	4445	
13	54.75	56.88	55.00	55.50	3571	1425	13871	6141	
14	55.50	59.00	55.00	57.38	1992	936	14807	7701	
15	57.38	57.75	55.63	56.00	1652	-1075	13732	8787	
16	56.00	56.38	55.50	55.88	2128	-290	13442	9625	
17	55.88	56.75	55.75	56.50	2927	1815	15257	10639	
18	56.50	57.00	53.75	54.00	3043	-2341	12916	11048	
19	54.00	54.50	51.88	53.00	2876	-1098	11818	11187	
20	53.00	54.50	51.50	52.25	2115	-529	11289	11205	
21	52.25	54.00	52.25	52.63	1831	397	11686	11292	
22	52.63	55.00	52.50	54.50	1237	925	12611	11529	Top
23	54.50	54.25	50.00	50.50	1410	-1327	11284	11485	No Sell
24	50.50	50.88	46.88	47.00	2065	-1806	9478	11123	signal
25	47.00	51.00	45.38	51.00	5712	4065	13543	11559	
26	51.00	51.75	49.75	51.00	3114	0	13543	11916	
27	51.00	53.25	49.75	53.00	2815	1609	15152	12499	
28	53.00	53.63	52.50	52.63	1231	-403	14749	12904	
29	52.63	53.38	50.50	53.38	2393	623	15372	13348	
30	53.38	55.88	53.38	55.00	2244	1454	16826	13974	
31	55.00	55.25	51.63	51.75	3376	-3030	13796	13942	

WORK SHEET

SYSTEM 23 (Method B)

LARRY WILLIAMS' ACCUMULATION/DISTRIBUTION METHOD

1 Weekly Open Price	2 Weekly High Price	3 Weekly Low Price	4 Weekly Close Price	5 Weekly Volume	6 $=\frac{4-1}{2-3}\times 5$ When Positive	7 $=\frac{4-1}{2-3}\times 5$ When Negative	8 10 Week Exponentially Smoothed Moving Average of Col. 6	9 10 Week Exponentially Smoothed Moving Average of Col. 7	
47.75	48.88	46.50	46.88	3085	0	1128			
46.88	47.38	45.63	46.25	2825	0	1017			
46.25	49.00	45.63	49.00	3778	3083	0			
49.00	50.75	48.75	49.75	4936	1851	0			
49.75	50.13	47.00	47.13	2711	0	2269			
47.13	48.50	46.88	48.13	3075	1898	0			
48.13	48.63	47.25	48.25	1955	170	0			
48.25	48.50	46.50	47.75	2021	0	505			
47.75	49.75	47.50	49.50	2011	1564	0			
49.50	50.25	49.25	49.50	8495	0	0	857	492	
49.50	51.38	49.25	51.38	4862	4291	0	1475	403	
51.38	55.00	51.00	54.75	5351	4508	0	2021	331	
54.75	56.88	55.00	55.50	3571	1425	0	1914	271	
55.50	59.00	55.00	57.38	1992	936	0	1738	222	
57.38	57.75	55.63	56.00	1652	0	1075	1425	376	
56.00	56.38	55.50	55.88	2128	0	290	1168	360	
55.88	56.75	55.75	56.50	2927	1815	0	1285	296	
56.50	57.00	53.75	54.00	3043	0	2341	1053	664	
54.00	54.50	51.88	53.00	2876	0	1098	864	742	
53.00	54.50	51.50	52.25	2115	0	529	708	704	
52.25	54.00	52.25	52.63	1831	397	0	652	577	
52.63	55.00	52.50	54.50	1237	925	0	701	473	
54.50	54.25	50.00	50.50	1410	0	1327	575	627	
50.50	(50.88)	46.88	47.00	2065	0	1806	(472)	(839)	Sell
47.00	51.00	(45.38)	51.00	5712	4065	0	(1118)	(688)	Buy
51.00	51.75	49.75	51.00	3114	0	0	917	564	
51.00	53.25	49.75	53.00	2815	1609	0	1042	463	
53.00	53.63	52.50	52.63	1231	0	403	854	452	
52.63	53.38	50.50	53.38	2393	623	0	813	371	
53.38	55.88	53.38	55.00	2244	1454	0	928	304	
55.00	55.25	51.63	51.75	3376	0	3030	761	795	

SYSTEM 24

DAVID BOSTIAN'S ACCUMULATION/DISTRIBUTION METHOD

GENERAL THEORY AND DISCUSSION:

(1)   Developed by David Bostian.

(2)   Determines Accumulation/Distribution by volume price change.

(3)   Intra-Day (or Intra-Week) Method.

(4)   Flow of Money $= \left(\dfrac{2C-H-L}{H-L} \right)$ V. where

C = Close H = High L = Low and V = Volume

Let's discuss three cases.

CASE I: When the stock closes at high.

Flow of Money $\quad = \quad \left(\dfrac{2C-H-L}{H-L} \right)$ V

Put C = H in the above formula.

$$\text{Flow of Money} \quad = \quad \left(\dfrac{2H-H-L}{H-L} \right) V$$

$$= \left(\dfrac{H-L}{H-L} \right) V$$

$$= \quad V$$

The total volume is assigned as positive or Buy volume.

CASE II: When the stock closes at low.

Flow of Money $\quad = \quad \left(\dfrac{2C-H-L}{H-L} \right)$ V

Put C = L in the above formula

$$\text{Flow of Money} \quad = \quad \left(\dfrac{2L-H-L}{H-L} \right) V$$

$$= \left(\dfrac{L-H}{H-L} \right) V$$

$$= \left(-\dfrac{H-L}{H-L} \right) V$$

$$= \quad -V$$

The total volume is assigned as negative or Sell volume.

CASE III: When the stock closes half way between high & low.

$$\text{Flow of Money} = \left(\frac{2C - H\text{-}L}{H\text{-}L} \right) V$$

Put C = H + L/2 in the above formula

$$\text{Flow of Money} = \left(\frac{2 \frac{H+L}{2} - H\ L}{H\text{-}L} \right) V$$

$$= \left(\frac{H+L - H\text{-}L}{H\text{-}L} \right) V$$

$$= 0$$

Buying and selling pressures are equal and, therefore, there is no flow of money.

(5)   The cumulative Flow of Money is calculated by adding daily (or weekly) Buying or selling pressure.

(6)   If the cumulative Flow of Money is positive, then the stock is under accumulation.

(7)   If the cumulative Flow of Money is negative, then the stock is under distribution.

(8)   Accumulated Flow of Money line is plotted under the price line.

(9)   Interpretation of the results is the same as Joseph Granville's On Balance volume, system 19.

SYSTEM DEFINITIONS: (METHOD A)

(1)   Col. 1 is the weekly high price.

(2)   Col. 2 is the weekly low price.

(3)   Col. 3 is the weekly close price.

(4)   Col. 4 is the weekly volume.

(5)   Col. 5 is calculated using formula $\left(\frac{2C - H\text{-}L}{H\text{-}L} \right) V$

(6)   Col. 6 is the accumulation of Col. 5.

(7)   Col. 7 is the 10 week exponentially smoothed moving average of Col. 6.

(8)   Buy signal is generated, when the bottom reversal point in Col. 7 exceeds by 6%.

(9)   Sell signal is generated, when the top reversal point in Col. 7 declines by 6%.

67

(10)　　　When a new Buy or Sell signal is generated, the old position is liquidated simultaneously. In other words, the system is always in the market.

SYSTEM DEFINITIONS (METHOD B)

(1)　　　Col. 1 is the weekly high price.

(2)　　　Col. 2 is the weekly low price.

(3)　　　Col. 3 is the weekly close price.

(4)　　　Col. 4 is the weekly volume.

(5)　　　Col. 5 is positive money flow when the value of formula is +.

(6)　　　Col. 6 is negative money flow when the value of formula is -.

(7)　　　Col. 7 is the 10 week ESMA of Col. 5.

(8)　　　Col. 8 is the 10 week ESMA of Col. 6.

(9)　　　Buy signal is generated, when the positive money flow (Col. 7) crosses negative money flow (Col. 8) on the upside by 6%.

(10)　　　Sell signal is generated, when the positive money flow (Col. 7) crosses negative money flow (Col. 8) on the downside by 6%.

(11)　　　When a new Buy or Sell signal is generated, the old position is liquidated simultaneously. Thus, the system is always in the market.

WORK SHEET

SYSTEM 24 (Method A)

DAVID BOSTIAN'S ACCUMULATION/DISTRIBUTION METHOD

	1 Weekly High Price H	2 Weekly Low Price L	3 Weekly Close Price C	4 Weeky Volume V	5 = (2C-H-L) / H-L x V	6 Accumulation of Col. 5	7 10 Week Exponentially Smoothed Moving Average of Col. 6	
1	48.88	46.50	46.88	3085	-2099	-2099		
2	47.38	45.63	46.25	2825	-823	-2922		
3	49.00	45.63	49.00	3778	3778	856		
4	50.75	48.75	49.75	4936	0	856		
5	50.13	47.00	47.13	2711	-2486	-1630		
6	48.50	46.88	48.13	3075	1670	40		
7	48.63	47.25	48.25	1955	878	918		
8	48.50	46.50	47.75	2021	505	1423		
9	49.75	47.50	49.50	2011	1564	2987		
10	50.25	49.25	49.50	8495	-425	2562	299	
11	51.38	49.25	51.38	4862	4862	7424	1582	
12	55.00	51.00	54.75	5351	4682	12106	3476	
13	56.88	55.00	55.50	3571	-1671	10435	4729	
14	59.00	55.00	57.38	1992	378	10813	5824	
15	57.75	55.63	56.00	1652	-1075	9738	6528	
16	56.38	55.50	55.88	2128	-290	9448	7054	
17	56.75	55.75	56.50	2927	1464	10912	7748	
18	57.00	53.75	54.00	3043	-2574	8338	7854	
19	54.50	51.88	53.00	2876	-417	7921	7866	Top
20	54.50	51.50	52.25	2115	-1058	6863	7686	
21	(54.00)	52.25	52.63	1831	-1036	5827	(7351)	Sell
22	55.00	52.50	54.50	1237	742	6569	7210	
23	54.25	50.00	50.50	1410	-1078	5491	6901	
24	50.88	46.88	47.00	2065	-1941	3550	6298	Bottom
25	51.00	(45.38)	51.00	5712	5712	9262	(6831)	Buy
26	51.75	49.75	51.00	3114	779	10041	7409	
27	53.25	49.75	53.00	2815	2413	12454	8317	
28	53.63	52.50	52.63	1231	-948	11506	8891	
29	53.38	50.50	53.38	2393	2393	13899	9793	
30	55.88	53.38	55.00	2244	664	14563	10651	
31	55.25	51.63	51.75	3376	3152	11411	10788	

WORK SHEET

SYSTEM 24 (Method B)

DAVID BOSTIAN'S ACCUMULATION/DISTRIBUTION METHOD

	1 Weekly High Price H	2 Weekly Low Price L	3 Weekly Close Price C	4 Weekly Volume Price V	5 = $\frac{(2C-H-L)}{H-L}$ When Positive	6 = V $\frac{(2C-H-L)}{H-L}$ When Negative	7 10 Week VExponentially Smoothed Moving Average of Col. 5	8 10 Week Exponentially Smoothed Moving Average of Col. 6	
1	48.88	46.50	46.88	3085	0	2099			
2	47.38	45.63	46.25	2825	0	823			
3	49.00	45.63	49.00	3778	3778	0			
4	50.75	48.75	49.75	4936	0	0			
5	50.13	47.00	47.13	2711	0	2486			
6	48.50	46.88	48.13	3075	1670	0			
7	48.63	47.25	48.25	1955	878	0			
8	48.50	46.50	47.75	2021	505	0			
9	49.75	47.50	49.50	2011	1564	0			
10	50.25	49.25	49.50	8495	0	425	840	583	
11	51.38	49.25	51.38	4862	4862	0	1564	478	
12	55.00	51.00	54.75	5351	4682	0	2125	392	
13	56.88	55.00	55.50	3571	0	1671	1742	622	
14	59.00	55.00	57.38	1992	378	0	1497	510	
15	57.75	55.63	56.00	1652	0	1075	1227	612	
16	56.38	55.50	55.88	2128	0	290	1006	554	
17	56.75	55.75	56.50	2927	1464	0	1089	454	
18	57.00	53.75	54.00	3043	0	2574	893	836	
19	54.50	51.88	53.00	2876	0	417	732	760	
20	(54.50)	51.50	52.25	2115	0	1058	(600)	(814)	Sell
21	54.00	52.25	52.63	1831	0	1036	492	854	
22	55.00	52.50	54.50	1237	742	0	537	700	
23	54.25	50.00	50.50	1410	0	1078	441	768	
24	50.88	46.88	47.00	2065	0	1941	361	979	
25	51.00	(45.38)	51.00	5712	5712	0	(1324)	(803)	Buy
26	51.75	49.75	51.00	3114.	779	0	1226	659	
27	53.25	49.75	53.00	2815	2413	0	1440	540	
28	53.63	52.50	52.63	1231	0	948	1181	613	
29	53.38	50.50	53.38	2393	2393	0	1399	503	
30	55.88	53.38	55.00	2244	664	0	1267	412	
31	55.25	51.63	51.75	3376	0	3152	1039	906	

SYSTEM 25

ULTRA HIGH VOLUME SYSTEM

THEORY AND DISCUSSION:

(1)   This system can be used with system 21 or any other similar volume system.

(2)   The latest volume of the stock should be at least 2.5 to 4.0 times the average volume of last 10 weeks.

(3)   The stocks can be selected from the most active list.

(4)   Stocks below $30 should show 12% to 15% price change within one to three weeks.

(5)   Stocks between $30 and $50 should show 10½% to 12% price change within one to three weeks.

(6)   Stocks between $50 and $100 should show 8% to 10% price change within one to three weeks.

(7)   Stocks above $100 should show 6% to 8% price change within one to three weeks.

SYSTEM 26

CROCKER'S PRICE/VOLUME METHOD

SYSTEM DEFINITIONS:

(1)   Developed by Benjamin Crocker and Diane W. Crocker.

(2)   Can be used on daily or weekly basis.

(3)   Weekly basis will work better than daily basis.

(4)   Put closing price on vertical scale.

(5)   Put volume on horizontal scale.

(6)   Draw straight line and arrow heads between successive points.

(7)   Buy signal is generated when a complete clockwise loop is formed.

        e.g.   clockwise.

(8)   Sell signal is generated when a complete counter clockwise loop is formed.

        e.g.   counter clockwise.

(9)   Works very well with strongly trended stocks with increasing volume.

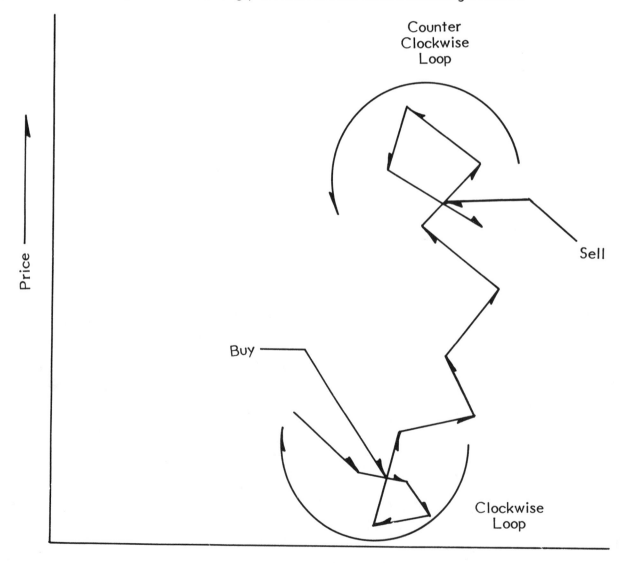

72

SYSTEM 27

MODIFIED INTERNAL INDEX

SYSTEM DEFINITIONS:

(1)   Col. 1 is the weekly closing price.

(2)   Compare the price this week with previous week.

        If the price has increased, put + in Col. 2.
        If the price has decreased, put - in Col. 2.
        If there is no change in price, put zero in Col. 2.

(3)   Col. 3 is the weekly volume.

(4)   Col. 4 is the 10 week exponentially smoothed moving avg. of Col. 3.

(5)   Put zero in Col. 5., if Col. 2 is negative or zero. Put volume in Col. 5, if Col. 2 is positive.

(6)   Col. 6 is the 10 week exponentially smoothed moving avg. of Col. 5.

(7)   Col. 7 = Internal Index = $\dfrac{\text{Col. 6}}{\text{Col. 4}} \times 100$

(8)   Col. 8 is the 8 week exponentially smoothed moving average of Col. 7.

(9)   Buy signal is generated when the value in Col. 8 crosses 53 on the upside.

(10)   Sell signal is generated when the value in Col. 8 crosses 47 on the downside.

(11)   When a new buy or sell signal is generated, the old position is liquidated simultaneously. In other words the system is always in the market.

GENERAL THEORY AND DISCUSSION:

(1)   Determine Accumulation/Distribution by comparing up volume with the total volume.

(2)   Inter-day or Inter-week method.

(3)   When the Internal Index crosses 50% line on the upside, there is net buying.

(4)   When the Internal Index crosses 50% line on the downside, there is net selling.

(5)   Mechanical Method of measuring Accumulation/Distribution by double filter.

	1	2	3	4	5	6	7	8
	Weekly Closing Price	Price Compared to Previous Price +, – or Zero	Weekly Volume	10 Week Exponentially Smoothed Moving Avg of Col. 3	Weekly Up Volume	10 Week Exponentially Smoothed Moving Avg of Col. 5	Col. 6 × 100 / Col. 4	8 Week Exponentially Smoothed Moving Avg of Col. 7
1	42.50		1259		1259			
2	43.13	+	1778		1778			
3	45.00	+	1438		1438			
4	45.25	+	1575		1575			
5	47.75	+	3085		3085			
6	46.88	–	2825		0			
7	46.25	–	3778		3778			
8	49.00	+	4936		4936			
9	49.75	+	2711		0			
10	47.13	–	3075	2646	0	1784	67.42	
11	48.13	+	1955	2522	1955	1815	71.97	
12	48.25	+	2021	2432	0	1488	61.18	
13	47.75	–	2011	2356	2011	1582	67.15	
14	49.50	+	8495	3461	0	1297	37.47	
15	49.50	0	4862	3713	4862	1939	52.22	
16	51.38	+	5351	4008	5351	2353	58.71	
17	54.75	+	3571	3929	3571	2736	69.64	60.72
18	56.50	+	1992	3581	0	2244	62.66	61.15
19	56.38	–	1652	3233	0	1840	56.91	60.21
20	56.00	–	2128	3034	0	1509	49.74	57.91
21	55.88	+	2927	3015	2927	1764	58.51	58.04
22	56.50	+	3043	3020	0	1447	47.91	55.81
23	54.00	–	2876	2994	0	1186	39.61	52.25
24	53.00	–	2115	2836	0	973	34.31	48.30
25	52.25	–						

WORK SHEET

SYSTEM 27

MODIFIED INTERNAL INDEX

	1 Weekly Closing Price	2 Price Compared to Previous Price +, - or Zero	3 Weekly Volume	4 10 Week Exponentially Smoothed Moving Avg of Col. 3	5 Weekly Up Volume	6 10 Week Exponentially Smoothed Moving Avg of Col. 5	7 Col. 6 × 100 / Col. 4	8 8 Week Exponentially Smoothed Moving Avg of Col. 7	
26	52.63	+	1831	2655	1831	1127	42.45	47.01	
27	54.50	+	1237	2400	1237	1147	47.79	47.19	
28	(50.50)	-	1410	2222	0	940	42.30	(46.11)	Sell
29	47.00	-	2065	2193	0	771	35.16	43.70	
30	51.00	+	5712	2827	5712	1661	58.75	47.01	
31	51.00	0	3114	2878	0	1362	47.32	47.08	
32	53.00	+	2815	2867	2815	1623	56.61	49.18	
33	52.63	-	1231	2573	0	1331	51.73	49.74	
34	53.38	+	2393	2540	2393	1522	59.92	51.98	
35	(55.00)	+	2244	2487	2244	1652	66.43	(55.16)	Buy
36	51.75	-	3376	2647	0	1355	51.19	54.28	

75

SYSTEM 28

REVERSAL INDEX

SYSTEM DEFINITIONS:

(1)   Developed by Edwin H. Tomkins.

(2)   Reversal Index = $\dfrac{\text{Daily or Weekly Volume}}{\text{High} - \text{Low}}$

(3)   This system is based on the assumption that there is usually high volume at the top and bottom.

(4)   When the stock/commodity is rising up, the high Reversal Index number means the price is likely to reverse the direction and go down. The greater the size of the Reversal Index, the stronger the signal.

(5)   When the stock/commodity price is going down, the high Reversal Index number means the price is likely to reverse direction and go up. The greater the size of the Reversal Index, the stronger the signal.

(6)   Don't use zero or very small number in the Denominator, because this will give you infinity or very large numbers. So use a minimum value of 0.25 for Denominator (stocks).

(7)   You could use 10 week exponentially smoothed moving average of Reversal Index to smooth out your data.

WORK SHEET

SYSTEM 28

REVERSAL INDEX

	1 High Price H	2 Low Price L	3 Close price C	4 Volume V	5 Reversal Index = $\frac{V}{H-L}$	
1	65.50	64.50	64.50	150	150	
2	64.50	64.00	64.25	275	550	
3	64.00	63.00	63.25	300	300	
4	63.00	61.50	61.50	700	467	
5	62.00	60.00	60.50	800	400	
6	60.00	58.00	58.50	1400	700	
7	59.00	57.00	57.25	2800	1400	
8	58.00	(56.00)	57.00	5600	(2800)	Buy
9	58.50	56.25	56.75	200	89	
10	59.50	57.50	58.00	300	150	
11	60.00	58.00	59.00	500	250	
12	62.00	60.50	61.00	800	533	
13	64.00	62.50	63.00	900	600	
14	65.00	64.50	64.75	1200	2400	
15	(65.00)	63.00	63.50	5000	(2500)	Sell

SYSTEM 29

DENSITY INDEX OR COUNTER TREND ANALYSIS

GENERAL THEORY AND DISCUSSION:

(1)   Employed by traders for many years.

(2)   Counter trend signals are obtained directly from price volume action of individual stocks.

(3)   Density Index is made by dividing the cumulative aggregate volume by the overall price range for the same time period. This represents the amount of volume necessary to move the stock one point in price.

(4)   When the stock/commodity price is rising up, the high density index means the price is likely to reverse the direction. This also suggests that the stock needs more volume to go up in price which is bearish.

(5)   When the stock/commodity price is going down, the high density index means the price is likely to reverse the direction. Since the stock/commodity needs more volume to go down, the stock/commodity is finding support at that level.

(6)   Circle the high & low of the trend once it is established.

(7)   Wait for the trend reversal, before beginning a new volume series.

(8)   You could use 10 week exponentially smoothed moving average of density index to smooth out your data.

SYSTEM DEFINITION:

(1)   Col. 1 is the high price.

(2)   Col. 2 is the low price.

(3)   Col. 3 is the close price.

(4)   Col. 4 is the price range. Price range is the maximum distance from high to low for a downtrend or low to high for an uptrend.

(5)   Col. 5 is the volume.

(6)   Col. 6 is accumulated volume for the downtrend.

(7)   Col. 7 is accumulated volume for the uptrend.

(8)   Col. 8 is the Density Index.

$$\text{Density Index} = \frac{\text{Accumulated Volume for Uptrend or Downtrend}}{\text{Range}}$$

(9)   Buy or sell signal is generated when the density Index becomes maximum.

(10)   When a new Buy or Sell signal is generated, the old position is liquidated simultaneously. In other words, the system is always in the market.

NOTE: Don't post volume data in Col. 6 or 7 if the direction of the trend is in doubt.

WORK SHEET

SYSTEM 29

DENSITY INDEX OR COUNTER TREND ANALYSIS

	1 High Price	2 Low Price	3 Close Price	4 Range	5 Volume	6 Accumulated Volume for Downtrend	7 Accumulated Volume for Uptrend	8 = Col. 6 or Col. 7 Range
1	65.50	64.50	64.50	1.00	150	150		150
2	64.50	64.00	64.25	1.50	275	425		283
3	64.00	63.00	63.25	2.50	300	725		290
4	63.00	61.50	61.50	4.00	700	1425		356
5	62.00	60.00	60.50	5.50	800	2225		406
6	60.00	58.00	58.50	7.50	1400	3625		483
7	59.00	57.00	57.25	8.50	2800	6425		756
8	58.00	(56.00)	57.00	9.50	5600	12025		(1266) Buy
9	58.50	56.25	56.75	2.50	200		200	80
10	59.50	57.50	58.00	3.50	300		500	143
11	60.00	58.00	59.00	4.00	500		1000	250
12	62.00	60.50	61.00	6.00	800		1800	300
13	64.00	62.50	63.00	8.00	900		2700	338
14	65.00	64.50	64.75	9.00	1200		3900	433
15	(65.00)	63.00	63.75	9.00	5000		8900	(989) Sell

80

EQUIVOLUME CHARTING

GENERAL THEORY AND DISCUSSION:

(1)   Was developed by Richard W. Arms Jr.

(2)   Represents volume and price more graphically than bar charts.

(3)   Range and volume are more significant for plotting on bar charts.

(4)   Price is plotted on vertical scale.

(5)   Volume is plotted on horizontal scale.

(6)   Two dimensional chart based on inter-day or inter-week price volume relationship.

(7)   Interpretation is very similar to bar chart.

(8)   Support and resistance levels can be studied.

(9)   Trend lines can also be drawn as with regular bar charts.

(10)   A very small price range on large volume will appear as a short and thick square or flat rectangle.

(11)   A large price spread on low volume will appear as a tall and thin rectangle.

(12)   Thick squares or flat rectangles indicate price reversal.

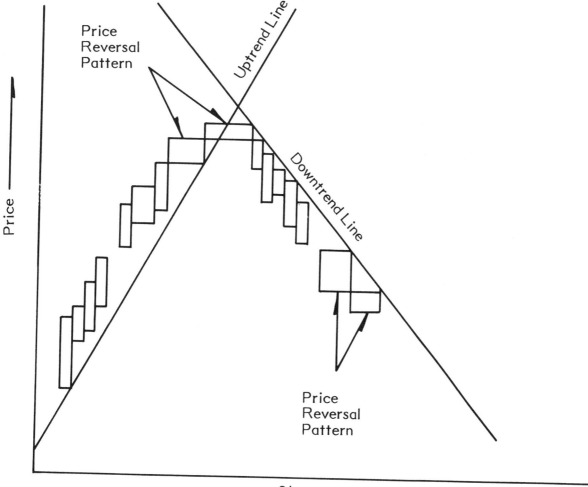

SYSTEM 31

VOLUME - GENERAL DISCUSSION

(1)

Prices	Volume	Effect
Rising	Rising	Bullish
Rising	Steady	Bullish
Rising	Declining	Bearish
Steady	Rising	Climax Turn
Steady	Steady	Neutral
Steady	Declining	Bullish
Declining	Rising	Bearish
Declining	Steady	Bearish
Declining	Declining	Bullish

(2) An advance starting on high or ultra-high volume is likely to lead to further gains.

(3) Strong volume should be the key to any stock/commodity selection.

(4) An advance continuing on dimishing volume is not likely to end but is showing loss of momentum.

(5) Diminishing volume during an advance does not represent a sell signal.

(6) Heavy volume following sustained advance without any appreciable price rise is a sign of price distribution.

(7) Heavy volume following upside break out is a sign of churning. The stock/commodity is testing the new high for a few days with advance being resumed later on.

(8) Heavy volume following a sustained decline without any appreciable price decline is a sign of accumulation.

(9) Heavy volume following downside break out is a sign of churning. The stock/commodity is testing the new low for a few days, with decline being resumed later on.

(10) Light volume on decline is usually neither bullish nor bearish.

(11) Light volume on decline is bullish under the following conditions:

(a)   When the light volume has persisted for some time - often weeks or months - the stock/commodity declines at a very slow rate.

(b)   Following a sharp run up on heavy volume, the stock/commodity backs off on diminishing volume for a few weeks. As soon as the heavy volume steps in again, the stock/commodity resumes its advance.

(12)   Light volume on a rally during a downtrend is a sign of decline in a few weeks.

SYSTEM 32

TRADING RANGE INDICATOR I

SYSTEM DEFINITIONS:

(1)   Col. 1 is the weekly high price.

(2)   Col. 2 is the weekly low price.

(3)   Col. 3 is the weekly close price.

(4)   Col. 4 is the average of high, low, and close = $\dfrac{H + L + C}{3}$ = (HLC) Avg.

(5)   Col. 5 = RCI = $\dfrac{\text{(HLC) Avg. this week - (HLC) Avg. one week ago}}{\text{(HLC) Avg. one week ago}}$

(6)   Sell signal is generated when the oscillator tops-out (successive higher readings followed by a lower reading) provided the oscillator reversal point is in the positive territory, e.g., 1.20, 1.25, 1.30, 1.35, 1.40, 1.37.

(7)   Buy signal is generated when the oscillator bottoms-out (successive lower readings followed by a higher reading) provided the oscillator reversal point is in the negative territory, e.g.,-1.20, -1.25, -1.30, -1.35, -1.40, -1.35.

(8)   When a new Buy or Sell signal is generated, the old position is liquidated simultaneously. In other words, the system is always in the market.

THEORY & DISCUSSION:

(1)   The rate of change is the amount of price change or % price change that has occured during a given time period.

(2)   The time period depends upon the cycles involved.

(3)   Rate of change = $\dfrac{\text{Cycle Length}}{2}$

Cycle length is measured by averaging two or three previous tops and bottoms.

(4)   For a ten day cycle, we have five day rate of change.

(5)   Five day dollar rate of change = closing Today - closing 5 days ago.

Also, 5 day % rate of change = $\dfrac{\text{Closing Today - Closing 5 days ago}}{\text{Closing 5 days ago}}$

(6)   Rate of change can be measured using closing, average of high and low, average of high, low and close or moving average of prices.

(7)

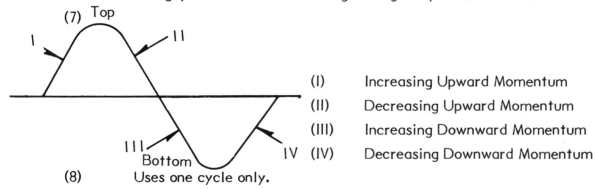

(I)   Increasing Upward Momentum

(II)   Decreasing Upward Momentum

(III)   Increasing Downward Momentum

(IV)   Decreasing Downward Momentum

(8)   Uses one cycle only.

WORK SHEET

SYSTEM 32

TRADING RANGE INDICATOR I

	1 Weekly High Price	2 Weekly Low Price	3 Weekly Close Price	4 Average of High, Low and Close	5 RC_I Based on Col. 4	
1	36.50	35.00	36.00	35.84		
2	37.00	35.50	36.50	36.34	1.40	
3	37.75	36.00	37.25	36.87	1.46	
4	38.00	37.00	37.50	37.50	1.75	Top
5	38.33	36.17	38.08	37.53	.08	Sell
6	39.08	36.83	37.17	37.69	.43	
7	40.75	37.00	39.00	38.92	3.26	
8	40.50	35.38	36.75	37.54	-3.55	
9	38.25	35.00	35.13	36.12	-3.78	Bottom
10	37.63	33.88	36.00	35.83	-.80	Buy
11	36.50	34.63	36.25	35.79	-.11	
12	36.00	35.50	35.75	35.75	-.11	
13	36.38	35.75	35.75	35.96	.59	
14	37.75	35.63	37.75	37.04	3.00	
15	39.38	37.50	38.25	38.38	3.62	Top
16	38.13	34.88	35.00	36.00	-6.20	Sell, Bottom
17	35.63	33.00	35.50	34.71	-3.58	Buy
18	36.00	34.38	35.00	35.13	1.21	
19	36.75	34.13	36.38	35.75	1.76	Top
20	36.88	35.63	36.50	36.34	1.65	Sell
21	37.00	35.75	36.25	36.33	-.03	Bottom
22	37.50	35.50	36.75	36.59	.72	Buy, Top
23	36.75	35.00	36.00	35.92	-1.83	Sell
24	36.00	34.75	35.00	35.25	-1.87	
25	35.00	33.25	34.50	34.25	-2.84	
26	33.00	32.25	32.75	32.67	-4.61	Bottom
27	33.25	33.00	33.00	33.09	1.29	Buy
28	34.50	33.50	34.25	34.09	3.02	Top
29	35.00	34.25	34.50	34.59	1.47	Sell
30	36.50	34.00	35.25	35.25	1.91	
31	37.00	34.25	36.75	36.00	2.13	

SYSTEM 33

TRADING RANGE INDICATOR 2

SYSTEM DEFINITIONS:

(1)   Col. 1 is the weekly high price.

(2)   Col. 2 is the weekly low price.

(3)   Col. 3 is the weekly close price.

(4)   Col. 4 is the average of high, low, and close = $\dfrac{H + L + C}{3}$ = (HLC) Avg.

(5)   Col. 5 = RC1 = $\dfrac{\text{(HLC) Avg. this week - (HLC) Avg. one week ago}}{\text{(HLC) Avg. one week ago}}$

(6)   Col. 6 is the same as Col. 4.

(7)   Col. 7 = RC3 = $\dfrac{\text{(HLC) Avg. this week - (HLC) Avg. three weeks ago}}{\text{(HLC) Avg. three weeks ago}}$

(8)   Col. 8 = Col. 5 + Col. 7.

(9)   Sell signal is generated when the oscillator tops-out (successive higher readings followed by a lower reading) provided the oscillator reversal point is in the positive territory, e.g,. 1.20, 1.25, 1.30, 1.35, (1.40,) 1.37.

(10)   Buy signal is generated when the oscillator bottoms-out (successive lower readings followed by a higher reading) provided the oscillator reversal point is in the negative territory, e.g., -1.20, -1.25, -1.30, -1.35, (-1.40,) -1.35.

(11)   When a new Buy or Sell signal is generated, the old position is liquidated simultaneously. In other words, the system is always in the market.

THEORY AND DISCUSSION:

(1)   Same as System 32.

(2)   Uses sum of two different cycles.

WORK SHEET

SYSTEM 33

TRADING RANGE INDICATOR 2

	1 Weekly High Price	2 Weekly Low Price	3 Weekly Close Price	4 Average of High Low and Close	5 RCI Based on Col. 4	6 Average of High Low and Close	7 RC3 Based on Col. 6	8 = RCI + RC3	
1	36.50	35.00	36.00	35.84		35.84			
2	37.00	35.50	36.50	36.34	1.40	36.34			
3	37.75	36.00	37.25	36.87	1.46	36.87			
4	38.00	37.00	37.50	37.50	1.75	37.50	4.63	6.34	
5	38.33	36.17	38.08	37.53	.08	37.53	3.27	3.35	
6	39.08	36.83	37.17	37.69	.43	37.69	2.22	2.65	
7	40.75	37.00	39.00	38.92	3.26	38.92	3.79	7.05	
8	40.50	35.00	36.75	37.54	-3.55	37.54	.03	-3.52	
9	38.25	35.00	35.13	36.12	-3.78	36.12	-4.17	-7.95	
10	37.63	33.88	36.00	35.83	-.80	35.83	-7.94	-8.74	Bottom
11	36.50	34.63	36.25	35.79	-.11	35.79	-4.66	-4.77	Buy
12	36.00	35.50	35.75	35.75	-.11	35.75	-1.02	-1.13	
13	36.38	35.75	35.75	35.96	.59	35.96	.36	.95	
14	37.75	35.63	37.75	37.04	3.00	37.04	3.49	6.49	
15	39.38	37.50	38.25	38.38	3.62	38.38	7.36	10.98	Top
16	38.13	34.88	35.00	36.00	-6.20	36.00	.11	-6.09	Sell
17	35.63	33.00	35.50	34.71	-3.58	34.71	-6.29	-9.87	Bottom
18	36.00	34.38	35.00	35.13	1.21	35.13	-8.47	-7.26	Buy
19	36.75	34.13	36.38	35.75	1.76	35.75	-.69	1.07	
20	36.88	35.63	36.50	36.34	1.65	36.34	4.70	6.35	Top
21	37.00	35.75	36.25	36.33	-.03	36.33	3.42	3.39	Sell
22	37.50	35.50	36.75	36.59	.72	36.59	2.35	3.07	
23	36.75	35.00	36.00	35.92	-1.83	35.92	-1.16	-2.99	
24	36.00	34.75	35.00	35.25	-1.87	35.25	-2.97	-4.84	
25	35.00	33.25	34.50	34.25	-2.84	34.25	-6.40	-9.24	
26	33.00	32.25	32.75	32.67	-4.61	32.67	-9.05	-13.66	Bottom
27	33.25	33.00	33.00	33.09	1.29	33.09	-6.13	-4.84	Buy
28	34.50	33.50	34.25	34.09	3.02	34.09	-.47	2.55	
29	35.00	34.25	34.50	34.59	1.47	34.59	5.88	7.35	
30	36.50	34.00	35.25	35.25	1.91	35.25	6.53	8.44	Top
31	37.00	34.25	36.00	36.00	2.13	36.00	5.60	7.73	Sell

87

SYSTEM 34

TRADING RANGE INDICATOR 3

SYSTEM DEFINITIONS:

(1)   Col. 1 is the weekly high price.

(2)   Col. 2 is the weekly low price.

(3)   Col. 3 is the weekly close price.

(4)   Col. 4 is the average of high, low, and close = $\dfrac{H + L + C}{3}$ = (HLC) Avg.

(5)   Col. 5 = RC1 = $\dfrac{\text{(HLC) Avg. this week - (HLC) Avg. one week ago}}{\text{(HLC) Avg. one week ago}}$

(6)   Col. 6 is the same as Col. 4.

(7)   Col. 7 = RC3 = $\dfrac{\text{(HLC) Avg. this week - (HLC) Avg. three weeks ago}}{\text{(HLC) Avg. three weeks ago}}$

(8)   Col. 8 is the same as Col. 4.

(9)   Col. 9 = RC5 = $\dfrac{\text{(HLC) Avg. this week - (HLC) Avg. five weeks ago}}{\text{(HLC) Avg. five weeks ago}}$

(10)   Col. 10 = Col. 5 + Col. 7 + Col. 9.

(11)   Sell signal is generated when the oscillator tops-out (successive higher readings followed by a lower reading) provided the oscillator reversal point is in the positive territory, e.g,. 1.20, 1.25, 1.30, 1.35, 1.40, 1.37.

(12)   Buy signal is generated when the oscillator bottoms-out (successive lower readings followed by a higher reading) provided the oscillator reversal point is in the negative territory, e.g., -1.20, -1.25, -1.30, -1.35, -1.40, -1.35.

(13)   When a new Buy or Sell signal is generated, the old position is liquidated simultaneously. In other words, the system is always in the market.

THEORY AND DISCUSSION:

(1)   Same as System 32.

(2)   Uses sum of three different time cycles.

WORK SHEET

SYSTEM 34

TRADING RANGE INDICATOR 3

	1	2	3	4	5	6	7	8	9	10	
	Weekly High Price	Weekly Low Price	Weekly Close Price	Avg of High, Low and Close	RC1 based on Col. 4	Avg of High, Low and Close	RC3 based on Col. 6	Avg of High, Low & Close	RC5 based on Col. 8	= RC 1 + RC 3 + RC 5	
1	36.50	35.00	36.00	35.84		35.84		35.84			
2	37.00	35.50	36.50	36.34	1.40	36.34		36.34			
3	37.75	36.00	37.25	36.87	1.46	36.87		36.87			
4	38.00	37.00	37.50	37.50	1.75	37.50	4.63	37.50			
5	38.33	36.17	38.08	37.53	.08	37.53	3.27	37.53			
6	39.08	36.83	37.17	37.69	.43	37.69	2.22	37.69	5.16	7.81	
7	40.75	37.00	39.00	38.92	3.26	38.92	3.79	38.92	7.10	14.15	Top Sell
8	40.50	35.00	36.75	37.54	-3.55	37.54	.03	37.54	1.82	-1.70	
9	38.25	35.00	35.13	36.12	-3.78	36.12	-4.17	36.12	-3.68	-11.63	
10	37.63	33.88	36.00	35.83	-.80	35.83	-7.94	35.83	-4.53	-13.26	Bottom Buy
11	36.50	34.63	36.25	35.79	-.11	35.79	-4.66	35.79	-5.04	-9.81	
12	36.00	35.50	35.75	35.75	-.11	35.75	-1.02	35.75	-8.14	-9.27	
13	36.38	35.75	35.75	35.96	.59	35.96	.36	35.96	-4.21	-3.26	
14	37.75	35.63	37.75	37.04	3.00	37.04	3.49	37.04	2.55	9.04	
15	32.38	37.50	38.25	38.38	3.62	38.38	7.36	38.38	7.12	18.10	Top Sell
16	38.13	34.88	35.00	36.00	-6.20	36.00	.11	36.00	.59	-5.50	
17	35.63	33.00	35.50	34.71	-3.58	34.71	-6.29	34.71	-2.91	-12.78	
18	36.00	34.38	35.00	35.13	1.21	35.13	-8.47	35.13	-2.31	-9.57	Bottom Buy
19	36.75	34.13	36.38	35.75	1.76	35.75	-.69	35.75	-3.48	-2.41	

89

WORK SHEET
SYSTEM 34
TRADING RANGE INDICATOR 3

	1	2	3	4	5	6	7	8	9	10	
	Weekly High Price	Weekly Low Price	Weekly Close Price	Avg of High, Low and Close	RC1 based on Col. 4	Avg of High, Low and Close	RC3 based on Col. 6	Avg of High, Low & Close	RC5 based on Col. 8	RC 1 + RC 3 + RC 5	
20	36.88	35.63	36.50	36.34	1.65	36.34	4.70	36.34	-5.32	1.03	
21	37.00	35.75	36.25	36.33	-0.03	36.33	3.42	36.33	.92	4.31	
22	37.50	35.50	36.75	36.59	.72	36.59	2.35	36.59	5.42	8.49	Top Sell
23	(36.75)	35.00	36.00	35.92	-1.83	35.92	-1.16	35.92	2.25	(-.74)	
24	36.00	34.75	35.00	35.25	-1.87	35.25	-2.97	35.25	-1.40	-6.24	
25	35.00	33.25	34.50	34.25	-2.84	34.25	-6.40	34.25	-5.75	-14.99	
26	33.00	32.25	32.75	32.67	-4.61	32.67	-9.05	32.67	-10.07	-23.73	Bottom Buy
27	33.25	(33.00)	33.00	33.09	1.29	33.09	-6.13	33.09	-9.57	(-14.41)	
28	34.50	33.50	34.25	34.09	3.02	34.09	-.47	34.09	-5.09	-2.54	
29	35.00	34.25	34.50	34.59	1.47	34.59	5.88	34.59	-1.87	5.48	
30	35.00	34.00	35.25	35.25	1.91	35.25	6.53	35.25	2.92	11.36	
31	37.00	34.25	36.75	36.00	2.13	36.00	5.60	36.00	10.19	17.92	Top Sell
32	(36.50)	35.00	35.25	35.58	-1.17	35.58	2.86	35.58	7.52	(9.21)	

SYSTEM 35

TRADING RANGE INDICATOR 4

SYSTEM DEFINITIONS:

(1)   Col. 1 is the weekly high price.

(2)   Col. 2 is the weekly low price.

(3)   Col. 3 is the weekly close price.

(4)   Col. 4 is the average of high, low, and close = $\dfrac{H + L + C}{3}$ = (HLC) Avg.

(5)   Col. 5 = RC1 = $\dfrac{\text{(HLC) Avg. this week - (HLC) Avg. one week ago}}{\text{(HLC) Avg. one week ago}}$

(6)   Col. 6 is the same as Col. 4.

(7)   Col. 7 = RC3 = $\dfrac{\text{(HLC) Avg. this week - (HLC) Avg. three weeks ago}}{\text{(HLC) Avg. three weeks ago}}$

(8)   Col. 8 is the same as Col. 4.

(9)   Col. 9 = RC5 = $\dfrac{\text{(HLC) Avg. this week - (HLC) Avg. five weeks ago}}{\text{(HLC) Avg. five weeks ago}}$

(10)   Col. 10 is the same as Col. 4.

(11)   Col. 11 = RC7 = $\dfrac{\text{(HLC) Avg. this week - (HLC) Avg. seven weeks ago}}{\text{(HLC) Avg. seven weeks ago}}$

(12)   Col. 12 = Col. 5 + Col. 7 + Col. 9 + Col. 11

(13)   Sell signal is generated when the oscillator tops-out (successive higher readings followed by a lower reading) provided the oscillator reversal point is in the positive territory, e.g,. 1.20, 1.25, 1.30, 1.35, 1.40, 1.37.

(14)   Buy signal is generated when the oscillator bottoms-out (successive lower readings followed by a higher reading) provided the oscillator reversal point is in the negative territory, e.g., -1.20, -1.25, -1.30, -1.35, -1.40, -1.35.

(15)   When a new Buy or Sell signal is generated, the old position is liquidated simultaneously. In other words, the system is always in the market.

THEORY AND DISCUSSION:

(1)   Same as System 32.

(2)   Uses sum of four different cycles.

WORK SHEET

SYSTEM 35

TRADING RANGE INDICATOR 4

	1	2	3	4	5	6	7	8	9	10	11	12	
	Weekly High Price	Weekly Low Price	Weekly Close Price	Avg of High, Low & Close	RC 1 based on Col. 4	Avg of High, Low & Close	RC 3 based on Col. 6	Avg of High, Low & Close	RC 5 based on Col. 8	Avg of High, Low & Close	RC 7 based on Col. 10	= RC 1 RC+3 RC+5 RC+7	
1	36.50	35.00	36.00	35.84		35.84		35.84		35.84			
2	37.00	35.50	36.50	36.34	1.40	36.34		36.34		36.34			
3	37.75	36.00	36.88	36.87	1.46	36.87	4.63	36.87		36.87			
4	38.00	37.00	37.50	37.50	1.75	37.50	3.27	37.50		37.50			
5	38.33	36.17	38.08	37.53	1.08	37.53	2.22	37.53		37.53			
6	39.08	36.83	37.17	37.69	.43	37.69	3.79	37.69	5.16	37.69			
7	40.75	37.00	39.00	38.92	3.26	38.92	.03	38.92	7.10	38.92	4.74		
8	40.50	35.00	37.17	37.54	-3.55	37.54	-4.17	37.54	1.82	37.54	-.61	3.04	
9	38.25	35.00	35.13	36.12	-3.78	36.12	-7.94	36.12	-3.68	36.12	-2.82	-12.24	
10	37.63	35.13	36.00	35.84	-.80	35.84	-4.66	35.84	-4.53	35.84	-4.56	-16.01	
11	36.50	33.88	36.25	35.79	-.11	35.79	-1.02	35.79	-5.04	35.79	-4.74	-14.37 (circled)	Bottom Buy
12	36.00	34.63 (circled)	35.75	35.75	-.11	35.75	-.11	35.75	-8.14	35.75	-4.74	-14.01	
13	36.38	35.50	35.75	35.96	.59	35.96	.36	35.96	-4.21	35.96	-7.85	-7.85	
14	37.75	35.63	37.75	37.04	3.00	37.04	3.49	37.04	2.55	37.04	4.21	4.21	
15	39.38	37.50	38.25	38.38	3.62	38.38	7.36	38.38	7.12	38.38	2.24	20.30	Top Sell
16	38.13 (circled)	34.88	35.00	36.00	-6.20	36.00	.11	36.00	.59	36.00	-.33	-5.83 (circled)	
17	35.63	33.00	35.00	34.71	-3.58	34.71	-6.29	34.71	-2.91	34.71	-3.13	-15.90	
18	36.00	34.13 (circled)	35.50	35.13	1.21	35.13	-8.47	35.13	-3.48	35.13	-1.84	-11.41 (circled)	Bottom Buy
19	36.75 (circled)	34.38 (circled)	36.38	35.75	1.76	35.75	-.69	35.75	-2.31	35.75	.00	-2.41	
20	36.88	35.00	36.50	36.34	1.65	36.34	4.70	36.34	-5.32	36.34	1.06	2.09	
21	37.00	35.63	36.25	36.33	-.03	36.33	3.42	36.33	.92	36.33	-1.92	2.39	
22	37.00	35.75	36.75	36.59	.72	36.59	2.35	36.59	5.42	36.59	-4.66	3.83	
23	36.75	35.50	36.00	35.92	-1.83	35.92	-1.16	35.92	2.25	35.92	-.22	-.96 (circled)	Top Sell
24	36.00	35.00	35.00	35.25	-1.87	35.25	-2.97	35.25	-1.40	35.25	1.56	-4.68	
25	35.00	33.25	34.50	34.25	-2.84	34.25	-6.40	34.25	-5.75	34.25	-2.50	-17.49	
26	33.00	32.25	32.75	32.67	-4.61	32.67	-9.05	32.67	-10.07	32.67	-8.62	-32.00	Bottom

SYSTEM 35

TRADING RANGE INDICATOR 4

	1	2	3	4	5	6	7	8	9	10	11	12	
	Weekly High Price	Weekly Low Price	Weekly Close Price	Avg of High, Low & Close	RC 1 based on Col. 4	Avg of High, Low & Close	RC 3 based on Col. 6	Avg of High, Low & Close	RC 5 based on Col. 8	Avg of High, Low & Close	RC 7 based on Col. 10	= RC 1 RC+3 RC+5 RC+7	
27	33.25	(33.00)	33.00	33.09	1.29	33.09	-6.13	33.09	-9.57	33.09	-8.94	(-23.35)	Buy
28	34.50	33.50	34.25	34.09	3.02	34.09	-.47	34.09	-5.09	34.09	-6.17	-8.71	
29	35.00	34.25	34.50	34.59	1.47	34.59	5.88	34.59	-1.87	34.59	-5.47	.41	
30	36.50	34.00	35.25	35.25	1.91	35.25	6.53	35.25	2.92	35.25	-1.87	9.49	
31	37.00	34.25	36.75	36.00	2.13	36.00	5.60	36.00	10.19	36.00	2.13	20.00	Top
32	(36.50)	35.00	35.25	35.58	-1.17	35.58	2.86	35.58	7.52	35.58	3.88	(13.09)	Sell

93

SYSTEM 36

SPECIAL MOMENTUM INDICATOR I

SYSTEM DEFINITIONS:

(1)　　　　Col. 1 is the weekly high price.

(2)　　　　Col. 2 is the weekly low price.

(3)　　　　Col. 3 is the weekly close price.

(4)　　　　Col. 4 is the average of high, low, and close = $\dfrac{H + L + C}{3}$ = (HLC) Avg.

(5)　　　　Col. 5 = RCI = $\dfrac{\text{(HLC) Avg. this week - (HLC) Avg. one week ago}}{\text{(HLC) Avg. one week ago}}$

(6)　　　　Col. 6 is the six week exponentially smoothed moving average of Col. 5.

(7)　　　　Sell signal is generated when the oscillator tops-out (successive higher readings followed by a lower reading) provided the oscillator reversal point is in the positive territory, e.g., 1.20, 1.25, 1.30, 1.35, 1.40, 1.37.

(8)　　　　Buy signal is generated when the oscillator bottoms-out (successive lower readings followed by a higher reading) provided the oscillator reversal point is in the negative territory, e.g., -1.20, -1.25, -1.30, -1.35, -1.40, -1.35.

(9)　　　　When a new Buy or Sell signal is generated, the old position is liquidated simultaneously. In other words, the system is always in the market.

THEORY AND DISCUSSION:

(1)　　　　Same as System 32.

WORK SHEET

SYSTEM 36

SPECIAL MOMENTUM INDICATOR I

	1	2	3	4	5	6	
	Weekly High Price	Weekly Low Price	Weekly Close Price	Average of High, Low and Close	RC I based on Col. 4	6 Week Expon. Smoothed moving Avg of Col. 5	
1	36.50	35.00	36.00	35.84			
2	37.00	35.50	36.50	36.34	1.40		
3	37.75	36.00	37.25	36.87	1.46		
4	38.00	37.00	37.50	37.50	1.75		
5	38.33	36.17	38.08	37.53	.08		
6	39.08	36.83	37.17	37.69	.43		
7	40.75	37.00	39.00	38.92	3.26	1.40	
8	40.50	35.00	36.75	37.54	-3.55	-.04	
9	38.25	35.00	35.13	36.12	-3.78	-1.12	Bottom
10	37.63	(33.88)	36.00	35.83	-.80	(-1.03)	Buy
11	36.50	34.63	36.25	35.79	-.11	-.76	
12	36.00	35.50	35.75	35.75	-.11	-.57	
13	36.38	35.75	35.75	35.96	.59	-.24	
14	37.75	35.63	37.75	37.04	3.00	.70	
15	39.38	37.50	38.25	38.38	3.62	1.55	Top
16	(38.13)	34.88	35.00	36.00	-6.20	(-.70)	Sell
17	35.63	33.00	35.50	34.71	-3.58	-1.53	Bottom
18	36.00	(34.38)	35.00	35.13	1.21	(-.74)	Buy
19	36.75	34.13	36.38	35.75	1.76	-.01	
20	36.88	35.63	36.50	36.34	1.65	.47	Top
21	(37.00)	35.75	36.25	36.33	-.03	(.32)	Sell
22	37.50	35.50	36.75	36.59	.72	.44	
23	36.75	35.00	36.00	35.92	-1.83	-.22	
24	36.00	34.75	35.00	35.25	-1.87	-.70	
25	35.00	33.25	34.50	34.25	-2.84	-1.32	
26	33.00	32.25	32.75	32.67	-4.61	-2.27	Bottom
27	33.25	(33.00)	33.00	33.09	1.29	(-1.24)	Buy
28	34.50	33.50	34.25	34.09	3.02	-.01	
29	35.00	34.25	34.50	34.59	1.47	.42	
30	36.50	34.00	35.25	35.25	1.91	.85	
31	37.00	34.25	36.75	36.00	2.13	1.22	Top
32	(36.50)	35.00	35.25	35.58	-1.17	(.53)	Sell

SYSTEM 37

SPECIAL MOMENTUM INDICATOR 2

SYSTEM DEFINITIONS:

(1)   Col. 1 is the weekly closing price.

(2)   Col. 2 is the 10 week exponentially smoothed moving average of Col. 1.

(3)   Col. 3 = RC5 = $\dfrac{\text{10 week MA this week - 10 week MA five weeks ago}}{\text{10 week MA five weeks ago}}$

(4)   Col. 4 = RC5 = $\dfrac{\text{Col. 3 Value this week - Col. 3 value five weeks ago}}{\text{Col. 3 value five weeks ago}}$

(5)   Sell signal is generated when both the oscillators in Col. 3 and Col. 4 top-out (successive higher readings followed by a lower reading) provided both the oscillator reversal points are in the positive territory, e.g., 1.20, 1.25, 1.30, 1.40, 1.35.

(6)   Buy signal is generated when both the oscillators in Col. 3 and Col. 4 bottom-out (Successive lower readings followed by a higher reading) provided both the oscillator reveral points are in the negative territory. e.g. -1.20, -1.30, -1.40, -1.10.

(7)   When a new Buy or Sell signal is generated, the old position is liquidated simultaneously. In other words, the system is always in the market.

THEORY AND DISCUSSION:

(1)   Same as System 32.

WORK SHEET

SYSTEM 37

SPECIAL MOMENTUM INDICATOR 2

	1	2	3	4	
	Weekly Closing Price	10 Week Exponentially Smoothed Moving Avg of Col. 1	RC 5 based on Col. 2	RC 5 based on Col. 3	
1	45.75	45.99			
2	46.00	45.99			
3	46.25	46.04			
4	46.75	46.17			
5	47.25	46.36			
6	48.00	46.66	.67		
7	47.00	46.72	.73		
8	48.50	47.04	1.00		
9	49.75	47.53	1.36		
10	50.25	48.02	1.66		
11	50.75	48.51	1.85	1.18	
12	51.00	48.96	2.24	1.51	Top
13	(49.00)	48.97	(1.93)	(.93)	Sell
14	49.00	48.98	1.45	.09	
15	48.00	48.80	.78	-.88	
16	47.50	48.57	.06	-1.79	
17	46.00	48.11	-.85	-3.09	
18	45.50	47.64	-1.33	-3.26	
19	44.75	47.12	-1.86	-3.31	
20	44.00	46.56	-2.24	-3.02	
21	44.00	46.09	-2.48	-2.54	Bottom
22	(44.50)	45.80	(-2.31)	(-1.46)	Buy
23	44.75	45.61	-2.03	-.70	

SYSTEM 38

SPECIAL MOMENTUM INDICATOR 3

SYSTEM DEFINITIONS:

(1)   Col. 1 is the weekly high price.

(2)   Col. 2 is the weekly low price.

(3)   Col. 3 is the weekly close price.

(4)   Col. 4 is the average of high, low, and close = $\dfrac{H + L + C}{3}$ = (HLC) Avg.

(5)   Col. 5 = RC3 = $\dfrac{\text{(HLC) Avg. this week - (HLC) Avg. three weeks ago}}{\text{(HLC) Avg. three weeks ago}}$

(6)   Col. 6 is the accumulation of all values in Col. 5.

(7)   Col. 7 = RC3 = $\dfrac{\text{Col. 6 Value this week - Col. 6 value three weeks ago}}{\text{Col. 6 value three weeks ago}}$

(8)   Sell signal is generated when the oscillator tops-out (successive higher readings followed by a lower reading) provided the oscillator reversal point is in the positive territory, e.g., 1.20, 1.25, 1.30, 1.35, 1.40, 1.37.

(9)   Buy signal is generated when the oscillator bottoms-out (successive lower readings followed by a higher reading) provided the oscillator reversal point is in the negative territory, e.g., -1.20, -1.25, -1.30, -1.35, -1.40, -1.35.

(10)   When a new Buy or Sell signal is generated, the old position is liquidated simultaneously. In other words, the system is always in the market.

THEORY AND DISCUSSION:

(1)   Same as System 32.

WORK SHEET

SYSTEM 38

SPECIAL MOMENTUM INDICATOR 3

	1	2	3	4	5	6	7	
	Weekly High Price	Weekly Low Price	Weekly Close Price	Average of High, Low and Close	RC 3 based on Col. 4	Accumu- lation of Col. 5	RC 3 based on Col. 6	
1	36.50	35.00	36.00	35.84				
2	37.00	35.50	36.50	36.34				
3	37.75	36.00	37.25	36.87				
4	38.00	37.00	37.50	37.50	1.66	1.66		
5	38.33	36.17	38.08	37.53	1.19	2.85		
6	39.08	36.83	37.17	37.69	.82	3.67		
7	40.75	37.00	39.00	38.92	1.42	5.09	3.43	
8	40.50	35.00	36.75	37.54	.01	5.10	2.25	
9	38.25	35.00	35.13	36.12	-1.57	3.53	-.14	
10	37.63	33.88	36.00	35.83	-3.09	.44	-4.65	
11	36.50	34.63	36.25	35.79	-1.75	-1.31	-6.41	Bottom
12	36.00	35.50	35.75	35.75	-.37	-1.68	-5.21	Buy
13	36.38	35.75	35.75	35.96	-.13	-1.55	-1.99	
14	37.75	35.63	37.75	37.04	1.25	-.30	1.01	
15	39.38	37.50	38.25	38.38	2.63	2.33	4.01	Top
16	38.13	34.88	35.00	36.00	.04	2.37	3.92	Sell
17	35.63	33.00	35.50	34.71	-2.33	.04	.34	
18	36.00	34.38	35.00	35.13	-3.25	-3.21	-5.54	
19	36.75	34.13	36.38	35.75	-.25	-3.46	-5.83	Bottom
20	36.88	35.63	36.50	36.34	1.63	-1.83	-1.87	Buy
21	37.00	35.75	36.25	36.33	1.20	-.63	2.58	
22	37.50	35.50	36.75	36.59	.84	.21	3.67	Top
23	36.75	35.00	36.00	35.92	-.42	-.21	1.62	Sell
24	36.00	34.75	35.00	35.25	-1.08	-1.29	-1.66	
25	35.00	33.25	34.50	34.25	-2.34	-3.63	-3.84	
26	33.00	32.25	32.75	32.67	-3.25	-6.88	-6.67	
27	33.25	33.00	33.00	33.09	-2.16	-9.04	-7.75	Bottom
28	34.50	33.50	34.25	34.09	-.16	-9.20	-5.57	Buy
29	35.00	34.25	34.50	34.59	1.92	-7.28	-.40	
30	36.50	34.00	35.25	35.25	2.16	-5.12	3.92	
31	37.00	34.25	36.75	36.00	1.91	-3.21	5.99	Top
32	36.50	35.00	35.25	35.58	.99	-2.22	5.06	Sell

SYSTEM 39

RELATIVE STRENGTH I

SYSTEM DEFINITIONS:

(1)   Col. 1 is the weekly closing price.

(2)   Col. 2 is the 10 week exponentially smoothed moving average of Col. 1.

(3)   Col. 3 = RC4 = $\dfrac{\text{10 week MA this Week - 10 week MA 4 weeks ago}}{\text{10 week MA 4 weeks ago}}$

(4)   Sell signal is generated when the oscillator tops-out (successive higher readings followed by a lower reading) provided the oscillator reversal point is in the positive territory, e.g., 1.20, 1.25, 1.30, 1.35, (1.40) 1.37.

(5)   Buy signal is generated when the oscillator bottoms-out (successive lower readings followed by a higher reading) provided the oscillator reversal point is in the negative territory, e.g., -1.20, -1.25, -1.30, -1.35, (-1.40) -1.35.

(6)   When a new Buy or Sell signal is generated, the old position is liquidated simultaneously. In other words, the system is always in the market.

THEORY AND DISCUSSION:

(1)   One of the most rigorously tested systems.

(2)   Stocks/commodities which are stronger than others, remain stronger in the near future too.

(3)   Stocks/commodities which are weaker than others, remain weaker in the near future too.

(4)   Basic theory is the same as System 32.

(5)   Uses one cycle only (Fixed moving average with one cycle).

WORK SHEET

SYSTEM 39

RELATIVE STRENGTH I

	1	2	3	
	Weekly Close Price	10 Week Exponentially Smoothed Moving Avg of Col. 1	RC 4 based on Col. 2	
1	49.00	47.88	1.79	
2	50.50	48.35	2.22	
3	51.50	48.92	3.25	
4	52.75	49.61	4.16	
5	54.00	50.40	5.26	
6	54.50	51.14	5.77	
7	56.00	52.01	6.32	
8	57.50	53.00	6.83	
9	59.00	54.08	7.30	
10	61.50	55.42	8.37	Top
11	60.00	56.24	8.13	Sell
12	62.50	57.37	8.25	
13	64.00	58.56	8.28	
14	62.75	59.32	7.04	
15	65.00	60.34	7.29	
16	64.00	61.00	6.33	
17	63.50	61.45	4.94	
18	64.00	61.91	4.37	
19	63.00	62.10	2.92	
20	62.50	62.18	1.93	
21	61.50	62.05	.98	
22	60.00	61.68	-.37	
23	59.50	61.29	-1.30	
24	58.00	60.70	-2.38	
25	57.50	60.12	-3.11	Bottom
26	58.50	59.83	-3.00	Buy
27	56.00	59.14	-3.51	
28	55.00	58.39	-3.81	
29	55.75	57.92	-3.66	
30	55.50	57.48	-3.93	
31	54.00	56.86	-3.86	
32	53.25	56.21	-3.73	

SYSTEM 40

RELATIVE STRENGTH 2

SYSTEM DEFINITIONS:

(1)   Col. I is the weekly closing price.

(2)   Col. 2 is the 10 week exponentially smoothed moving average of Col. I.

(3)   Col. 3 = RC4 = $\dfrac{\text{10 week MA this Week - 10 week MA 4 weeks ago}}{\text{10 week MA 4 weeks ago}}$

(4)   Col. 4 is the same as Col. 2

(5)   Col. 5 = RC8 = $\dfrac{\text{10 week MA this Week - 10 week MA 8 weeks ago}}{\text{10 week MA 8 weeks ago}}$

(6)   Col. 6 = Col. 3 + Col. 5.

(7)   Sell signal is generated when the oscillator tops-out (successive higher readings followed by a lower reading) provided the oscillator reversal point is in the positive territory, e.g., 1.20, 1.25, 1.30, 1.35, 1.40, 1.37.

(8)   Buy signal is generated when the oscillator bottoms-out (successive lower readings followed by a higher reading) provided the oscillator reversal point is in the negative territory, e.g., -1.20, -1.25, -1.30, -1.35, -1.40, -1.35.

(9)   When a new Buy or Sell signal is generated, the old position is liquidated simultaneously. In other words, the system is always in the market.

THEORY AND DISCUSSION:

(1)   Same as System 39.

(2)   Uses two different cycles (Fixed moving average with two different cycles).

WORK SHEET

SYSTEM 40

RELATIVE STRENGTH 2

	1	2	3	4	5	6	
	Weekly Close Price	10 Week Exponentially Smoothed Moving Avg of Col. 1	RC 4 based on Col. 2	10 Week Exponentially Smoothed Moving Avg of Col. 1	RC 8 based on Col. 4	= RC 4 + RC 8	
1	49.00	47.88	1.79	47.88	3.46	5.25	
2	50.50	48.35	2.22	48.35	3.78	6.00	
3	51.50	48.92	3.25	48.92	4.73	7.98	
4	52.75	49.61	4.16	49.61	5.69	9.85	
5	54.00	50.40	5.26	50.40	7.14	12.40	
6	54.50	51.14	5.77	51.14	8.12	13.89	
7	56.00	52.01	6.32	52.01	9.77	16.09	
8	57.50	53.00	6.83	53.00	11.27	18.10	
9	59.00	54.08	7.30	54.08	12.95	20.25	
10	61.50	55.42	8.37	55.42	14.62	22.99	
11	60.00	56.24	8.13	56.24	14.94	23.09	
12	62.50	57.37	8.25	57.37	15.64	23.89	
13	64.00	58.56	8.28	58.56	16.19	24.47	Top
14	62.75	59.32	7.04	59.32	16.00	23.04	Sell
15	65.00	60.34	7.29	60.34	16.02	23.31	
16	64.00	61.00	6.33	61.00	15.09	21.42	
17	63.50	61.45	4.94	61.45	13.63	18.57	
18	64.00	61.91	4.37	61.91	11.71	16.08	
19	63.00	62.10	2.92	62.10	10.42	13.34	
20	62.50	62.18	1.93	62.18	8.38	10.31	
21	61.50	62.05	.98	62.05	5.96	6.94	
22	60.00	61.68	-.37	61.68	3.98	3.61	
23	59.50	61.29	-1.30	61.29	1.57	.27	
24	58.00	60.70	-2.38	60.70	-.49	-2.87	
25	57.50	60.12	-3.11	60.12	-2.16	-5.27	
26	58.50	59.83	-3.00	59.83	-3.36	-6.36	
27	56.00	59.14	-3.51	59.14	-4.77	-8.28	
28	55.00	58.39	-3.81	58.39	-6.10	-9.91	
29	55.75	57.92	-3.66	57.92	-6.66	-10.32	
30	55.50	57.48	-3.93	57.48	-6.81	-10.74	
31	54.00	56.86	-3.86	56.86	-7.23	-11.09	
32	53.25	56.21	-3.73	56.21	-7.40	-11.13	Bottom

103

SYSTEM 41

RELATIVE STRENGTH 3

SYSTEM DEFINITIONS:

(1)   Col. 1 is the weekly closing price.

(2)   Col. 2 is the 10 week exponentially smoothed moving average of Col. 1.

(3)   Col. 3 = RC4 = $\dfrac{\text{10 week MA this Week - 10 week MA 4 weeks ago}}{\text{10 week MA 4 weeks ago}}$

(4)   Col. 4 is the same as Col. 2.

(5)   Col. 5 = RC8 = $\dfrac{\text{10 week MA this Week - 10 week MA 8 weeks ago}}{\text{10 week MA 8 weeks ago}}$

(6)   Col. 6 is the same as Col. 2.

(7)   Col. 7 = RC12 = $\dfrac{\text{10 week MA this Week - 10 week MA 12 weeks ago}}{\text{10 week MA 12 weeks ago}}$

(8)   Col. 8 = Col. 3 + Col. 5 + Col. 7.

(9)   Sell signal is generated when the oscillator tops-out (successive higher readings followed by a lower reading) provided the oscillator reversal point is in the positive territory, e.g., 1.20, 1.25, 1.30, 1.35, 1.40, 1.37.

(10)   Buy signal is generated when the oscillator bottoms-out (successive lower readings followed by a higher reading) provided the oscillator reversal point is in the negative territory, e.g., -1.20, -1.25, -1.30, -1.35, -1.40, -1.35.

(11)   When a new Buy or Sell signal is generated, the old position is liquidated simultaneously. In other words, the system is always in the market.

THEORY AND DISCUSSION:

(1)   Same as System 39.

(2)   Uses three different cycles (Fixed moving average with three different cycles).

WORK SHEET

SYSTEM 41

RELATIVE STRENGTH 3

	1 Weekly Close Price	2 10 Week Exponentially Smoothed Moving Avg of Col. 1	3 RC 4 based on Col. 2	4 10 Week Exponentially Smoothed Moving Avg of Col. 1	5 RC 8 based on Col. 4	6 10 Week Exponentially Smoothed Moving Avg of Col. 1	7 RC 12 based on Col. 6	8 = RC 4 + RC 8 + RC 12	
1	49.00	47.88	1.79	47.88	3.46	47.88	5.46	10.71	
2	50.50	48.35	2.22	48.35	3.78	48.35	6.03	12.03	
3	51.50	48.92	3.25	48.92	4.73	48.92	6.70	14.68	
4	52.75	49.61	4.16	49.61	5.69	49.61	7.82	17.67	
5	54.00	50.40	5.26	50.40	7.14	50.40	8.90	21.30	
6	54.50	51.14	5.77	51.14	8.12	51.14	9.77	23.66	
7	56.00	52.01	6.32	52.01	9.77	52.01	11.35	27.44	
8	57.50	53.00	6.83	53.00	11.27	53.00	12.91	31.01	
9	59.00	54.08	7.30	54.08	12.95	54.08	14.97	35.22	
10	61.50	55.42	8.37	55.42	14.62	55.42	17.17	40.16	
11	60.00	56.24	8.13	56.24	14.96	56.24	18.70	41.79	
12	62.50	57.37	8.25	57.37	15.64	57.37	20.45	44.34	
13	64.00	58.56	8.28	58.56	16.19	58.56	22.31	46.78	Top
14	62.75	59.32	7.04	59.32	16.00	59.32	22.69	45.73	Sell
15	65.00	60.34	7.29	60.34	16.02	60.34	23.34	46.65	
16	64.00	61.00	6.33	61.00	15.09	61.00	22.96	44.38	
17	63.50	61.45	4.94	61.45	13.63	61.45	21.92	40.49	
18	64.00	61.91	4.37	61.91	11.71	61.91	21.06	37.14	
19	63.00	62.10	2.92	62.10	10.42	62.10	19.40	32.74	
20	62.50	62.18	1.93	62.18	8.38	62.18	17.32	27.63	
21	61.50	62.05	.98	62.05	5.96	62.05	14.74	21.68	
22	60.00	61.68	-.37	61.68	3.98	61.68	11.30	14.90	
23	59.50	61.29	-1.30	61.29	1.57	61.29	8.98	9.25	

WORK SHEET
SYSTEM 41
RELATIVE STRENGTH 3

	1 — Weekly Close Price	2 — 10 Week Exponentially Smoothed Moving Avg of Col. 1	3 — RC 4 based on Col. 2	4 — 10 Week Exponentially Smoothed Moving Avg of Col. 1	5 — RC 8 based on Col. 4	6 — 10 Week Exponentially Smoothed Moving Avg of Col. 1	7 — RC 12 based on Col. 6	8 — RC 4 + RC 8 + RC 12 =
24	58.00	60.70	-2.38	60.70	-.49	60.70	5.80	2.93
25	57.50	60.12	-3.11	60.12	-2.16	60.12	2.66	-2.61
26	58.50	59.83	-3.00	59.83	-3.36	59.83	.86	-5.50
27	56.00	59.14	-3.51	59.14	-4.77	59.14	-1.99	-10.27
28	55.00	58.39	-3.81	58.39	-6.10	58.39	-4.28	-14.19
29	55.75	57.92	-3.66	57.92	-6.66	57.92	-5.74	-16.06
30	55.50	57.48	-3.93	57.48	-6.81	57.48	-7.16	-17.90
31	54.00	56.86	-3.86	56.86	-7.23	56.86	-8.44	-19.53
32	53.50	56.21	-3.73	56.21	-7.40	56.21	-9.60	-20.73
33	53.25	55.72	-3.80	55.72	-7.32	55.72	-10.20	-21.32
34	52.50	55.14	-4.07	55.14	-7.84	55.14	-10.60	-22.51
35	51.00	54.40	-4.33	54.40	-8.01	54.40	-11.24	-23.58
36	50.00	53.60	-4.64	53.60	-8.20	53.60	-11.70	-24.54
37	50.00	52.78	-5.28	52.78	-8.87	52.78	-12.21	-26.36
38	49.00	51.92	-5.84	51.92	-9.67	51.92	-13.22	-28.73
39	48.00	51.03	-6.19	51.03	-10.25	51.03	-13.71	-30.15
40	47.00	50.40	-5.97	50.40	-10.34	50.40	-13.68	-29.99
	(47.50)							Bottom Buy

106

SYSTEM 42

RELATIVE STRENGTH 4

(1) Col. I is the weekly closing price.

Col. 2 is the 10 week exponentially smoothed moving average of Col. I.

(3) $\text{Col. 3} = RC4 = \dfrac{\text{10 week MA this Week - 10 week MA 4 weeks ago}}{\text{10 week MA 4 weeks ago}}$

(4) Col. 4 is the same as Col. 2.

(5) $\text{Col. 5} = RC8 = \dfrac{\text{10 week MA this Week - 10 week MA 8 weeks ago}}{\text{10 week MA 8 weeks ago}}$

(6) Col. 6 is the same as Col. 2.

(7) $\text{Col. 7} = RC12 = \dfrac{\text{10 week MA this Week - 10 week MA 12 weeks ago}}{\text{10 week MA 12 weeks ago}}$

(8) Col. 8 is the same as Col. 2.

(9) $\text{Col. 9} = RC16 = \dfrac{\text{10 week MA this Week - 10 week MA 16 weeks ago}}{\text{10 week MA 16 weeks ago}}$

(10) Col. 10 = Col. 3 + Col. 5 + Col. 7 + Col. 9.

(11) Sell signal is generated when the oscillator tops-out (successive higher readings followed by a lower reading) provided the oscillator reversal point is in the positive territory, e.g., 1.20, 1.25, 1.30, 1.35, (1.40,) 1.37.

(12) Buy signal is generated when the oscillator bottoms-out (successive lower readings followed by a higher reading) provided the oscillator reversal point is in the negative territory, e.g., -1.20, -1.25, -1.30, -1.35, (-1.40,) -1.35.

(13) When a new Buy or Sell signal is generated, the old position is liquidated simultaneously. In other words, the system is always in the market.

THEORY AND DISCUSSION:

(1) Same as System 39.

(2) Uses four different cycles. (Fixed moving average with four different cycles).

WORK SHEET

SYSTEM 42

RELATIVE STRENGTH 4

	1	2	3	4	5	6	7	8	9	10	
	Weekly Close Price	10 Week Exponentially Smooth Moving Avg of Col. 1	RC 4 based on Col. 2	10 Week Exponentially Smooth Moving Avg of Col. 1	RC 8 based on Col. 4	10 Week Exponentially Smooth Moving Avg of Col. 1	RC 12 based on Col. 6	10 Week Exponentially Smooth Moving Avg of Col. 1	RC 16 based on Col. 8	= RC 4 + RC 8 + RC 12 + RC 16	
1	49.00	47.88	1.79	47.88	3.46	47.88	5.46	47.88	6.40	17.11	
2	50.50	48.35	2.22	48.35	3.78	48.35	6.03	48.35	7.33	19.36	
3	51.50	48.92	3.25	48.92	4.73	48.92	6.70	48.92	8.30	22.98	
4	52.75	49.61	4.16	49.61	5.69	49.61	7.82	49.61	9.47	27.14	
5	54.00	50.40	5.26	50.40	7.14	50.40	8.90	50.40	11.01	32.31	
6	54.50	51.14	5.77	51.14	8.12	51.14	9.77	51.14	12.15	35.81	
7	56.00	52.01	6.32	52.01	9.77	52.01	11.35	52.01	13.44	40.88	
8	57.50	53.00	6.83	53.00	11.27	53.00	12.91	53.00	15.19	46.20	
9	59.00	54.08	7.30	54.08	12.95	54.08	14.97	54.08	16.85	52.07	
10	61.50	55.42	8.37	55.42	14.62	55.42	17.17	55.42	18.95	59.11	
11	60.00	56.24	8.13	56.24	14.96	56.24	18.70	56.24	20.40	62.19	
12	62.50	57.37	8.25	57.37	15.64	57.37	20.45	57.37	22.22	66.56	
13	64.00	58.56	8.28	58.56	16.19	58.56	22.31	58.56	24.49	71.27	Top
14	62.75	59.32	7.04	59.32	16.00	59.32	22.69	59.32	25.41	71.14	Sell
15	65.00	60.34	7.29	60.34	16.02	60.34	23.34	60.34	27.35	74.00	
16	64.00	61.00	6.33	61.00	15.09	61.00	22.96	61.00	28.07	72.45	
17	63.50	61.45	4.94	61.45	13.63	61.45	21.92	61.45	28.34	68.83	
18	64.00	61.91	4.37	61.91	11.71	61.91	21.06	61.91	28.05	65.19	
19	63.00	62.10	2.92	62.10	10.42	62.10	19.40	62.10	26.94	59.68	
20	62.50	62.18	1.93	62.18	8.38	62.18	17.32	62.18	25.34	52.97	
21	61.50	62.05	.98	62.05	5.96	62.05	14.74	62.05	23.12	44.80	
22	60.00	61.68	-.37	61.68	3.98	61.68	11.30	61.68	20.61	35.52	
23	59.50	61.29	-1.30	61.29	1.57	61.29	8.98	61.29	17.84	27.09	
24	58.00	60.70	-2.38	60.70	-.49	60.70	5.80	60.70	14.53	17.46	
25	57.50	60.12	-3.11	60.12	-2.16	60.12	2.66	60.12	11.17	8.56	

WORK SHEET

SYSTEM 42

RELATIVE STRENGTH 4

	1	2	3	4	5	6	7	8	9	10
	Weekly Close Price	10 Week Exponentially Smooth Moving Avg of Col. 1	RC 4 based on Col. 2	10 Week Exponentially Smooth Moving Avg of Col. 1	RC 8 based on Col. 4	10 Week Exponentially Smooth Moving Avg of Col. 1	RC 12 based on Col. 6	10 Week Exponentially Smooth Moving Avg of Col. 1	RC 16 based on Col. 8	= $RC\,4$ RC^+8 RC^+12 RC^+16
26	58.50	59.83	-3.00	59.83	-3.36	59.83	.86	59.83	7.96	2.46
27	56.00	59.14	-3.51	59.14	-4.77	59.14	-1.99	59.14	5.16	-5.11
28	55.00	58.39	-3.81	58.39	-6.10	58.39	-4.28	58.39	1.78	-12.41
29	55.75	57.92	-3.66	57.92	-6.66	57.92	-5.74	57.92	-1.09	-17.15
30	55.50	57.48	-3.93	57.48	-6.81	57.48	-7.16	57.48	-3.10	-21.00
31	54.00	56.86	-3.86	56.86	-7.23	56.86	-8.44	56.86	-5.77	-25.30
32	53.25	56.21	-3.73	56.21	-7.40	56.21	-9.60	56.21	-7.85	-28.58
33	53.50	55.72	-3.80	55.72	-7.32	55.72	-10.20	55.72	-9.32	-30.64
34	52.50	55.14	-4.07	55.14	-7.84	55.14	-10.60	55.14	-10.94	-33.45
35	51.00	54.40	-4.33	54.40	-8.01	54.50	-11.24	54.40	-12.40	-35.98
36	50.00	53.60	-4.64	53.60	-8.20	53.60	-11.70	53.60	-13.80	-38.34
37	49.00	52.78	-5.28	52.78	-8.87	52.78	-12.21	52.78	-14.94	-41.30
38	48.00	51.92	-5.84	51.92	-9.67	51.92	-13.22	51.92	-15.82	-44.55
39	47.00	51.03	-6.19	51.03	-10.25	51.03	-13.71	51.03	-16.74	-46.89
40	47.50	50.40	-5.97	50.40	-10.34	50.40	-13.68	50.40	-16.97	-46.96
41	46.00	49.61	-6.01	49.61	-10.97	49.61	-14.35	49.61	-17.48	-48.81
42	46.50	49.05	-5.53	49.05	-11.04	49.05	-14.67	49.05	-18.02	-49.26
43	45.50	48.41	-5.13	48.41	-11.01	48.41	-14.86	48.41	-18.14	-49.14
44	44.00	47.62	-5.52	47.62	-11.16	47.62	-15.28	47.62	-18.44	-50.40
45	43.00	46.79	-5.68	46.79	-11.35	46.79	-16.03	46.79	-19.22	-52.28

Bottom Buy (Col. 10, row 43: -49.14 circled; Col. 1, row 43: 45.50 circled)

109

SYSTEM 43

RELATIVE STRENGTH 5

(1)   Col. I is the weekly closing price.

(2)   Col. 2 is the 5 week exponentially smoothed moving average of Col. I.

(3)   Col. 3 = RC3 = $\dfrac{\text{5 week MA this Week - 5 week MA 3 weeks ago}}{\text{5 week MA 3 weeks ago}}$

(4)   Sell signal is generated when the oscillator tops-out (successive higher readings followed by a lower reading) provided the oscillator reversal point is in the positive territory, e.g., 1.20, 1.25, 1.30, 1.35, 1.40, 1.37.

(5)   Buy signal is generated when the oscillator bottoms-out (successive lower readings followed by a higher reading) provided the oscillator reversal point is in the negative territory, e.g., -1.20, -1.25, -1.30, -1.35, -1.40, -1.35.

(6)   When a new Buy or Sell signal is generated, the old position is liquidated simultaneously. In other words, the system is always in the market.

THEORY AND DISCUSSION:

(1)   Same as System 39.

(2)   One moving average with one cycle.

WORK SHEET

SYSTEM 43

RELATIVE STRENGTH 5

	1	2	3	
	Weekly Close Price	5 Week Exponentially Smoothed Moving Avg of Col. 1	RC 3 based on Col. 2	
1	59.00	56.34	6.83	
2	60.00	57.55	6.93	
3	61.50	58.85	6.94	Top
4	(62.50)	60.06	(6.60)	Sell
5	63.00	61.03	6.05	
6	63.50	61.84	5.08	
7	64.25	62.64	4.30	
8	63.00	62.76	2.83	
9	65.00	63.50	2.68	
10	64.00	63.66	1.63	
11	63.50	63.61	1.35	
12	64.00	63.74	.38	
13	63.00	63.49	-.27	
14	62.50	63.17	-.69	
15	61.50	62.62	-1.76	
16	60.00	61.75	-2.74	
17	59.50	61.01	-3.42	
18	58.00	60.02	-4.15	
19	57.50	59.19	-4.15	
20	56.25	58.22	-4.57	Bottom
21	(55.75)	57.40	(-4.37)	Buy

SYSTEM 44

RELATIVE STRENGTH 6

SYSTEM DEFINITIONS:

(1)   Col. 1 is the weekly closing price.

(2)   Col. 2 is the 5 week exponentially smoothed moving average of Col. 1.

(3)   Col. 3 = RC3 = $\dfrac{\text{5 week MA this Week - 5 week MA 3 weeks ago}}{\text{5 week MA 3 weeks ago}}$

(4)   Col. 4 is the 10 week exponentially smoothed moving average of Col. 1.

(5)   Col. 5 = RC6 = $\dfrac{\text{10 week MA this Week - 10 week MA 6 weeks ago}}{\text{10 week MA 6 weeks ago}}$

(6)   Col. 6 = Col. 3 + Col. 5.

(7)   Sell signal is generated when the oscillator tops-out (successive higher readings followed by a lower reading) provided the oscillator reversal point is in the positive territory, e.g., 1.20, 1.25, 1.30, 1.35, 1.40, 1.37.

(8)   Buy signal is generated when the oscillator bottoms-out (successive lower readings followed by a higher reading) provided the oscillator reversal point is in the negative territory, e.g., -1.20, -1.25, -1.30, -1.35, -1.40, -1.35.

(9)   When a new Buy or Sell signal is generated, the old position is liquidated simultaneously. In other words, the system is always in the market.

THEORY AND DISCUSSION:

(1)   Same as System 39.

(2)   Two moving averages with two different cycles.

WORK SHEET

SYSTEM 44

RELATIVE STRENGTH 6 .

	1	2	3	4	5	6	
	Weekly Close Price	5 Week Exponentially Smoothed Moving Avg of Col. 1	RC 3 based on Col. 2	10 Week Exponentially Smoothed Moving Avg of Col. 1	RC 6 based on Col. 4	= RC 3 RC + 6	
1	59.00	56.34		54.09			
2	60.00	57.55	6.93	55.16	11.12	18.05	
3	61.50	58.85	6.94	56.30	11.66	18.60	
4	62.50	60.06	6.60	57.41	12.22	18.82	Top
5	63.00	61.03	6.03	58.42	12.28	18.33	Sell
6	63.50	61.84	5.08	59.33	11.92	17.00	
7	64.25	62.64	4.30	60.22	11.33	15.63	
8	63.00	62.76	2.83	60.72	10.08	12.91	
9	65.00	63.50	2.68	61.49	9.22	11.90	
10	64.00	63.66	1.63	61.94	7.89	9.52	
11	63.50	63.61	1.35	62.22	6.50	7.85	
12	64.00	63.74	.38	62.54	5.41	5.79	
13	63.00	63.49	-.27	62.62	3.99	3.72	
14	62.50	63.17	-.69	62.60	3.10	2.41	
15	61.50	62.62	-1.76	62.40	1.48	-.28	
16	60.00	61.75	-2.74	61.97	.05	-2.69	
17	59.50	61.01	-3.42	61.53	-1.11	-4.53	
18	58.00	60.02	-4.15	60.89	-2.64	-6.79	
19	57.50	59.19	-4.15	60.28	-3.74	-7.89	
20	56.25	58.22	-4.57	59.55	-4.87	-9.44	
21	55.75	57.40	-4.37	58.87	-5.66	-10.03	
22	54.00	56.28	-4.92	57.99	-6.42	-11.34	Bottom
23	54.50	55.69	-4.35	57.36	-6.78	-11.13	Buy
24	54.00	55.13	-3.95	56.76	-6.78	-10.73	

SYSTEM 45

RELATIVE STRENGTH 7

SYSTEM DEFINITIONS:

(1)   Col. 1 is the weekly closing price.

(2)   Col. 2 is the 5 week exponentially smoothed moving average of Col. 1.

(3)   Col. 3 = RC3 = $\dfrac{\text{5 week MA this Week - 5 week MA 3 weeks ago}}{\text{5 week MA 3 weeks ago}}$

(4)   Col. 4 is the 10 week exponentially smoothed moving average of Col. 1.

(5)   Col. 5 = RC6 = $\dfrac{\text{10 week MA this Week - 10 week MA 6 weeks ago}}{\text{10 week MA 6 weeks ago}}$

(6)   Col. 6 is the 15 week exponentially smoothed moving average of Col. 1.

(7)   Col. 7 = RC9 = $\dfrac{\text{15 week MA this Week - 15 week MA 9 weeks ago}}{\text{15 week MA 9 weeks ago}}$

(8)   Col. 8 = Col. 3 + Col. 5 + Col. 7.

(9)   Sell signal is generated when the oscillator tops-out (successive higher readings followed by a lower reading) provided the oscillator reversal point is in the positive territory, e.g., 1.20, 1.25, 1.30, 1.35, 1.40, 1.37.

(10)   Buy signal is generated when the oscillator bottoms-out (successive lower readings followed by a higher reading) provided the oscillator reversal point is in the negative territory, e.g.,-1.20, -1.25, -1.30, -1.35, -1.40, -1.35.

(11)   When a new Buy or Sell signal is generated, the old position is liquidated simultaneously. In other words, the system is always in the market.

THEORY AND DISCUSSION:

(1)   Same as System 39.

(2)   Three moving averages with three different time cycles.

WORK SHEET

SYSTEM 45

RELATIVE STRENGTH 7

	1	2	3	4	5	6	7	8
	Weekly Close Price	5 Week Exponentially Smoothed Moving Avg of Col. 1	RC 3 based on Col. 2	10 Week Exponentially Smoothed Moving Avg of Col. 1	RC 6 based on Col. 4	15 Week Exponentially Smoothed Moving Avg of Col. 1	RC 9 based on Col. 6	= RC 3 + RC 6 + RC 9
1	59.00	56.34		54.09				
2	60.00	57.55	6.93	55.16	11.12	53.65	13.35	31.40
3	61.50	58.85	6.94	56.30	11.66	54.67	14.52	33.12
4	62.50	60.06	6.60	57.41	12.22	55.69	15.47	34.29
5	63.00	61.03	6.05	58.42	12.28	56.64	16.02	34.35
6	63.50	61.84	5.08	59.33	11.92	57.53	16.25	33.25 Top Sell
7	64.25	62.64	4.30	60.22	11.33	58.40	16.47	32.10
8	63.00	62.76	2.83	60.72	10.08	59.00	15.91	28.82
9	65.00	63.50	2.68	61.49	9.22	59.78	15.49	27.39
10	64.00	63.66	1.63	61.94	7.89	60.33	14.48	24.00
11	63.50	63.61	1.35	62.22	6.50	60.74	13.22	21.07
12	64.00	63.74	.38	62.54	5.41	61.17	11.89	17.68
13	63.00	63.49	-.27	62.62	3.99	61.40	10.25	13.97
14	62.50	63.17	-.69	62.60	3.10	61.55	8.67	11.08
15	61.50	62.62	-1.76	62.40	1.48	61.54	6.97	6.69
16	60.00	61.75	-2.74	61.97	.05	61.34	5.03	2.34
17	59.50	61.01	-3.42	61.53	-1.11	61.10	3.56	-.97
18	58.00	60.02	-4.15	60.89	-2.64	60.70	1.54	-5.25
19	57.50	59.19	-4.15	60.28	-3.74	60.28	-.08	-7.97
20	56.25	58.22	-4.57	59.55	-4.87	59.76	-1.61	-11.05
21	55.75	57.40	-4.37	58.87	-5.66	59.24	-3.16	-13.19
22	54.00	56.28	-4.92	57.99	-6.42	58.56	-4.63	-15.97
23	54.50	55.69	-4.35	57.36	-6.78	58.03	-5.72	-16.85
24	54.00	55.13	-3.95	56.76	-6.78	57.51	-6.55	-17.28
25	53.50	54.60	-2.99	56.17	-6.82	56.99	-7.09	-16.90 Bottom Buy
26	53.25	54.15	-2.77	55.65	-6.55	56.50	-7.53	-16.85

115

SYSTEM 46

RELATIVE STRENGTH 8

SYSTEM DEFINITIONS:

(1)   Col. 1 is the weekly closing price.

(2)   Col. 2 is the 5 week exponentially smoothed moving average of Col. 1.

(3)   Col. 3 = RC3 = $\dfrac{\text{5 week MA this Week - 5 week MA 3 weeks ago}}{\text{5 week MA 3 weeks ago}}$

(4)   Col. 4 is the 10 week exponentially smoothed moving average of Col. 1.

(5)   Col. 5 = RC6 = $\dfrac{\text{10 week MA this Week - 10 week MA 6weeks ago}}{\text{10 week MA 6 weeks ago}}$

(6)   Col. 6 is the 15 week exponentially smoothed moving average of Col. 1.

(7)   Col. 7 = RC9 = $\dfrac{\text{15 week MA this Week - 15 week MA 9 weeks ago}}{\text{15 week MA 9 weeks ago}}$

(8)   Col. 8 is the 20 week exponentially smoothed moving average of Col. 1.

(9)   Col. 9 = RC12 = $\dfrac{\text{20 week MA this Week - 20 week MA 12 weeks ago}}{\text{20 week MA 12 weeks ago}}$

(10)   Col. 10 = Col. 3 + Col. 5 + Col. 7 + Col. 9.

(11)   Sell signal is generated when the oscillator tops-out (successive higher readings followed by a lower reading) provided the oscillator reversal point is in the positive territory, e.g., 1.20, 1.25, 1.30, 1.35, 1.40, 1.37.

(12)   Buy signal is generated when the oscillator bottoms-out (successive lower readings followed by a higher reading) provided the oscillator reversal point is in the negative territory, e.g., -1.20, -1.25, -1.30, -1.35, -1.40, -1.35.

(13)   When a new Buy or Sell signal is generated, the old position is liquidated simultaneously. In other words, the system is always in the market.

THEORY AND DISCUSSION:

(1)   Same as System 39.

(2)   Four moving averages with four different cycles.

WORK SHEET

SYSTEM 46

RELATIVE STRENGTH 8

	1	2	3	4	5	6	7	8	9	10
	Weekly Close Price	5 Week Exponentially Smooth Moving Avg of Col. 1	RC 3 based on Col. 2	10 Week Exponentially Smooth Moving Avg of Col. 1	RC 6 based on Col. 4	15 Week Exponentially Smooth Moving Avg of Col. 1	RC 9 based on Col. 6	20 Week Exponentially Smooth Moving Avg of Col. 1	RC12 based on Col. 8	= RC 3 RC+6 RC+9 RC+12 Top Sell
1	59.00	56.34	6.93	54.09	11.12	53.65	13.35	52.40	16.35	50.64
2	60.00	57.55	6.94	55.16	11.66	54.67	14.52	53.31	17.63	51.98
3	61.50	58.85	6.60	56.30	12.22	55.69	15.47	54.23	18.51	(51.76)
4	62.50	60.06	6.05	57.41	12.28	56.64	16.02	55.11	19.19	51.29
5	63.00	61.03	5.08	58.42	11.92	57.53	16.25	55.95	19.21	48.03
6	(63.50)	61.84	4.30	59.33	11.33	58.40	16.47	56.78	19.33	46.72
7	64.25	62.64	2.83	60.22	10.08	59.00	15.91	57.40	19.12	43.12
8	63.00	62.76	2.68	60.72	9.22	59.78	15.49	58.16	18.49	39.56
9	65.00	63.50	1.63	61.49	7.89	60.33	14.49	58.74	17.68	35.36
10	64.00	63.66	1.35	61.94	6.50	60.74	13.22	59.22	16.43	30.40
11	63.50	63.61	.38	62.22	5.41	61.17	11.89	59.70	15.04	26.12
12	64.00	63.74	-.27	62.54	3.99	61.40	10.25	60.03	13.30	19.99
13	63.00	63.49	-.69	62.62	3.10	61.55	8.67	60.28	11.30	13.64
14	62.50	63.17	-1.76	62.60	1.48	61.54	6.97	60.40	9.24	8.27
15	61.50	62.62	-2.74	62.40	.05	61.34	5.03	60.36	7.33	2.08
16	60.00	61.75	-3.42	61.97	-1.11	61.10	3.56	60.20	5.30	-2.67
17	59.50	61.01	-4.15	61.53	-2.64	60.70	1.54	60.05	3.55	-7.50
18	58.00	60.02	-4.15	60.89	-3.74	60.28	-.08	59.79	1.56	-11.60
19	57.50	59.19	-4.57	60.28	-4.87	59.76	-1.61	59.44	-.31	-16.28
20	56.25	58.22	-4.37	59.55	-5.66	59.24	-3.16	59.07	-1.79	-18.64
21	55.75	57.40	-4.92	58.87	-6.42	58.56	-4.63	58.56		
22	54.00	56.28	-4.35	57.99	-6.78	58.03	-5.72	58.16		
23	54.50	55.69		57.36						

WORK SHEET
SYSTEM 46

RELATIVE STRENGTH 8

	1	2	3	4	5	6	7	8	9	10
	Weekly Close Price	5 Week Exponentially Smooth Moving Avg of Col. 1	RC 3 based on Col. 2	10 Week Exponentially Smooth Moving Avg of Col. 1	RC 6 based on Col. 4	15 Week Exponentially Smooth Moving Avg of Col. 1	RC 9 based on Col. 6	20 Week Exponentially Smooth Moving Avg of Col. 1	RC 12 based on Col. 8	RC 3 = RC+6 RC+9 RC+12
24	54.00	55.13	-3.95	56.76	-6.78	57.51	-6.55	57.74	-3.28	-20.56
25	53.50	54.60	-2.99	56.17	-6.82	56.99	-7.09	57.32	-4.51	-21.41
26	53.25	54.15	-2.77	55.65	-6.55	56.50	-7.53	56.91	-5.59	-22.44
27	52.00	53.44	-3.07	54.99	-6.59	55.91	-7.89	56.42	-6.59	-24.14
28	51.13	52.68	-3.52	54.30	-6.36	55.29	-8.28	55.89	-7.41	-25.57
29	50.00	51.79	-4.36	53.52	-6.69	54.60	-8.63	55.30	-8.14	-26.82
30	50.75	51.45	-3.72	53.02	-6.59	54.10	-8.68	54.85	-8.66	-27.65 Bottom
31	50.00	50.97	-3.25	52.48	-6.57	53.57	-8.52	54.36	-9.08	-27.42 Buy

SYSTEM 47

DUNNIGAN'S THRUST METHOD

UPTREND AND TOP:

Uptrend begins when the current high and low prices rise above the corresponding high and low prices of the lowest downtrend day. The highest price is called the top.

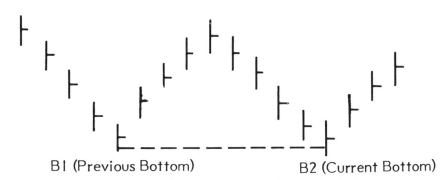

DOWNTREND AND BOTTOM:

Downtrend begins when the current high and low prices decline below the corresponding high and low prices of the highest day in the uptrend. The lowest price is called the bottom.

After defining uptrend and downtrend, we will set-up Buy and Sell patterns:

	Buy Patterns:		Sell Patterns:
1.	Test of Bottom (TOB)	6.	Test of Top (TOT)
2.	Closing Price Reversal (CPR)	7.	Closing Price Reversal (CPR)
3.	Narrow Range (NR)	8.	Narrow Range (NR)
4.	Inside Range (IR)	9.	Inside Range (IR)
5.	Penetration of Top (PT)	10.	Penetration of Bottom (PB)

1. Test of Bottom (TOB)

When the bottom price in the downtrend is within 2% of the previous one or two bottoms, test of bottom exists.

2.   <u>Closing Price Reversal (CPR)</u> is present when the closing price on the lowest range day in the current downtrend is above the closing price of the previous day.

(a)   Lowest range day in downtrend
(b)   Closing price on the lowest range day is above the previous closing price

3.   <u>Narrow Range (NR)</u>.   A Narrow Range is ½ or less of the largest daily range in the current downtrend.

(a)   NR is present because this range is 1/2 or less of the largest range

<u>Inside Range (IR)</u> is present when the range for the day is within the price range of the previous day.

(a)   IR is present because this range is within the previous range

5.   <u>Penetration of Top (PT)</u> is present when the price rises above previous top (or last top).

Top T1

PT is present

120

6. <u>Test of Top (TOT)</u>. When the top price in the current uptrend is within 2% of the previous one or two tops, Test of Top exists.

7. <u>Closing Price Reversal (CPR)</u> is present when the closing price on the highest range day in the current uptrend is below the previous closing price.

8. <u>Narrow Range (NR)</u> is same as narrow range in Buy patterns.

9. <u>Inside Range (IR)</u> is same as inside range in Buy patterns.

10. <u>Penetration of Bottom (PB)</u> is present when the price declines below the previous bottom (or last bottom).

<u>Buy signal is generated</u>, when:

a. Two or more of the buy patterns are present.

b. When the current high price exceeds the highest price of the lowest day in downtrend by an amount equal to the average of last 4 days ranges.

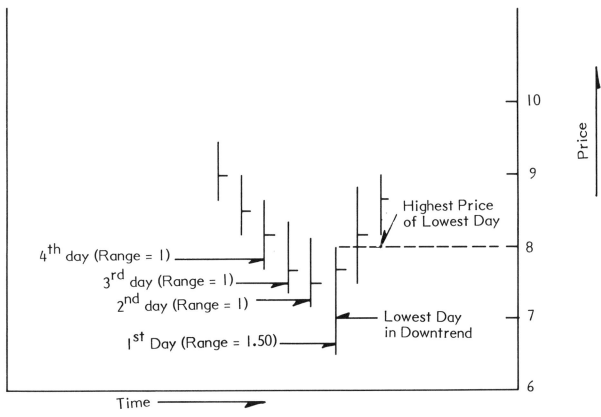

$$\text{Buy Signal Price} = 8 + \frac{1.50 + 1.00 + 1.00 + 1.00}{4}$$

$$= 8 + 1.13$$

$$= 9.13$$

Buy Signal will be generated above 9.13

121

<u>Sell signal is generated</u>, when:

a.   Two or more of the sell patterns are present.

b.   When the current low price declines below the lowest price of the highest day in uptrend by an amount equal to the average of the last 4 days ranges.

When a new Buy or Sell signal is generated, the old position is liquidated simultaneously. In other words, the system is always in the market.

SYSTEM 48

DUNNIGAN'S ONE WAY FORMULA

Since the Thrust Method was slightly too sensitive, some of the false signals can be eliminated using one way formula.

Buy signal is generated, when

1. Two or more Buy patterns as discussed in Thrust Method are present.

2. When the current low price is completely above the high of the lowest range day in the downtrend.

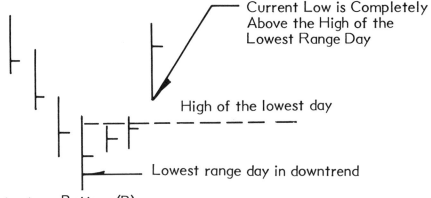

Sell signal is generated, when Bottom (B)

1. Two or more Sell patterns as discussed in Thrust Method are present.

2. When the current high price is completely below the low price of the highest range day in the uptrend.

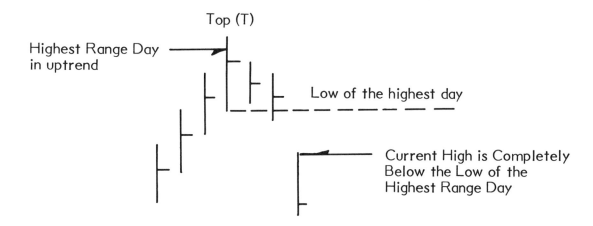

123

SYSTEM 49

COLE METHOD

GENERAL THEORY AND DISCUSSION:

I. Developed by George Cole.

2. Method of Entry or Exit once you have determined you want to buy long or sell short.

3. Take the highest range day in a rally. Average high, low and close. From this average price subtract the range (high - low) for the day. This gives the value below which one can buy; e.g., high 36, low 34, close 35.

Average price = $\dfrac{36 + 35 + 34}{3}$ = 35   Range = 36 - 34 = 2

Buy price = 35 - 2 = 33. Thus, 33 or below is the price at which one should buy.

4. Buy price remains the same until the high is exceeded.

5. Take the lowest range day in a decline. Average high, low and close. To this average price, add the range (high - low) for the day. This gives the value above which one should sell short; e.g., high 36, low 34, close 35.

Average price = $\dfrac{36 + 35 + 34}{3}$ = 35   Range = 36 - 34 = 2

Sell short price = 35 + 2 = 37. Thus, 37 or above is the price at which one should sell short.

SYSTEM 50

DONCHIAN'S TWO WEEK CHANNEL

SYSTEM DEFINITIONS:

(I)   Rule I: A Buy signal is generated whenever the price exceeds the high of the previous two weeks.

(2)   Rule 2:   A Sell signal is generated whenever the price declines below the low of the previous two weeks.

(3)   When a new Buy or Sell signal is generated, the old position is liquidated simultaneously. In other words, the system is always in the market.

APPLICABLE FOR

(I)   Soybean Oil

(2)   Hogs

(3)   Cattle

(4)   Pork Bellies

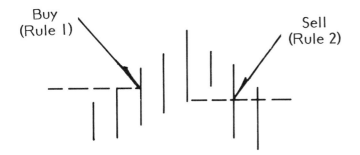

DONCHIAN'S MODIFIED TWO WEEK CHANNEL

SYSTEM DEFINITIONS:

(1)   Rule 1:   A Buy signal is generated whenever the price exceeds the high of the previous two weeks.

(2)   Rule 2:   A Sell signal is generated whenever the price declines below the low of the previous two weeks.

(3)   Rule 3:   Close out long position, if the price falls below the low of the previous one week.

(4)   Rule 4:   Cover your short position, if the price exceeds the high of the previous one week.

(5)   The added advantage of the modified system is that it will keep you out of the market some of the time.

APPLICABLE FOR

(1)   Soybean Oil

(2)   Hogs

(3)   Cattle

(4)   Pork Bellies

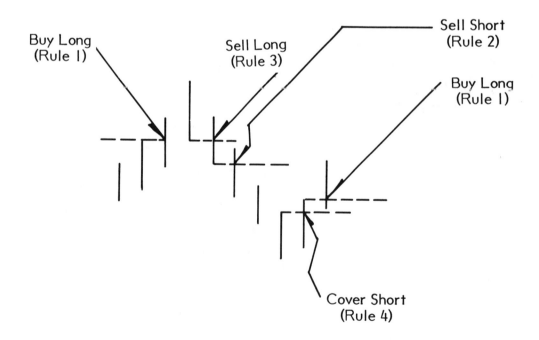

SYSTEM 52

DONCHIAN'S THREE WEEK CHANNEL

SYSTEM DEFINITIONS:

(1)   Rule 1:   A Buy signal is generated whenever the price exceeds the high of the previous three weeks.

(2)   Rule 2:   A Sell signal is generated whenever the price declines below the low of the previous three weeks.

(3)   When a new Buy or Sell signal is generated, the old position is liquidated simultaneously. In other words, the system is always in the market.

APPLICABLE FOR

(1)   Soybeans

(2)   Soybean Meal

(3)   Wheat

(4)   Sugar

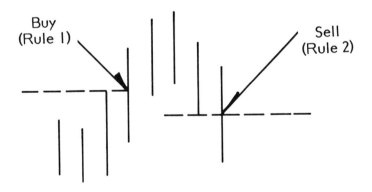

SYSTEM 53

DONCHIAN'S MODIFIED THREE WEEK CHANNEL

SYSTEM DEFINITIONS:

(1)   Rule 1:   A Buy signal is generated whenever the price exceeds the high of the previous three weeks.

(2)   Rule 2:   A Sell signal is generated whenever the price declines below the low of the previous three weeks.

(3)   Rule 3:   Close out long position, if the price falls below the low of the previous one week.

(4)   Rule 4:   Cover your short position, if the price exceeds the high of the previous one week.

(5)   The added advantage of the modified system is that it will keep you out of the market some of the time.

APPLICABLE FOR

(1)   Soybeans

(2)   Soybean Meal

(3)   Wheat

(4)   Sugar

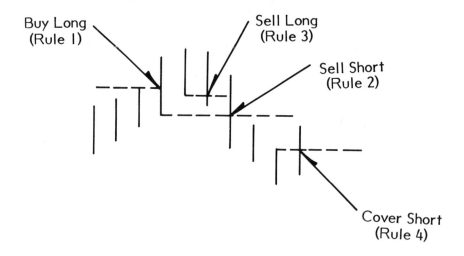

SYSTEM 54

DONCHIAN'S FOUR WEEK CHANNEL

SYSTEM DEFINITIONS:

(1)   Rule 1:   A Buy signal is generated whenever the price exceeds the high of the previous four weeks.

(2)   Rule 2:   A Sell signal is generated whenever the price declines below the low of the previous four weeks.

(3)   When a new Buy or Sell signal is generated, the old position is liquidated simultaneously. In other words, the system is always in the market.

APPLICABLE FOR

(1)   Cotton

(2)   Interest rates and currencies

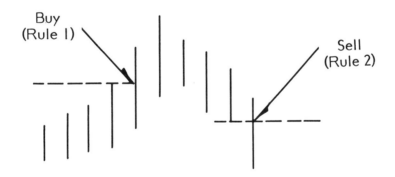

SYSTEM 55

DONCHIAN'S MODIFIED FOUR WEEK CHANNEL

SYSTEM DEFINITIONS:

(1)   Rule 1:   A Buy signal is generated whenever the price exceeds the high of the previous four weeks.

(2)   Rule 2:   A Sell signal is generated whenever the price declines below the low of the previous four weeks.

(3)   Rule 3:   Close out long position, if the price falls below the low of the previous two weeks.

(4)   Rule 4:   Cover your short position, if the price exceeds the high of the previous two weeks.

(5)   The added advantage of the modified system is that it will keep you out of the market some of the time.

APPLICABLE FOR

(1)   Cotton

(2)   Interest rates and currencies

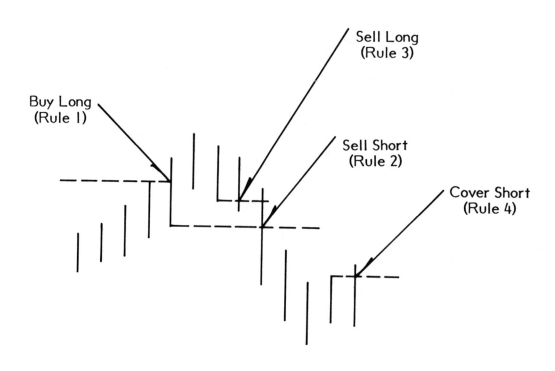

130

SYSTEM 56

DONCHIAN'S FIVE WEEK CHANNEL

SYSTEM DEFINITIONS:

(1)   Rule 1:   A Buy signal is generated whenever the price exceeds the high of the previous five weeks.

(2)   Rule 2:   A Sell signal is generated whenever the price declines below the low of the previous five weeks.

(3)   When a new Buy or Sell signal is generated, the old position is liquidated simultaneously. In other words, the system is always in the market.

APPLICABLE FOR

(1)   Corn

(2)   Cocoa

(3)   Plywood

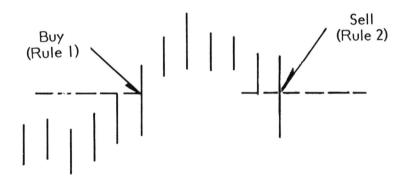

SYSTEM 57

DONCHIAN'S MODIFIED FIVE WEEK CHANNEL

SYSTEM DEFINITIONS:

(1)   Rule 1:   A Buy signal is generated whenever the price exceeds the high of the previous five weeks.

(2)   Rule 2:   A Sell signal is generated whenever the price declines below the low of the previous five weeks.

(3)   Rule 3:   Close out long position, if the price falls below the low of the previous two weeks.

(4)   Rule 4:   Cover your short position, if the price exceeds the high of the previous two weeks.

(5)   The added advantage of the modified system is that it will keep you out of the market some of the time.

APPLICABLE FOR

(1)   Corn

(2)   Cocoa

(3)   Plywood

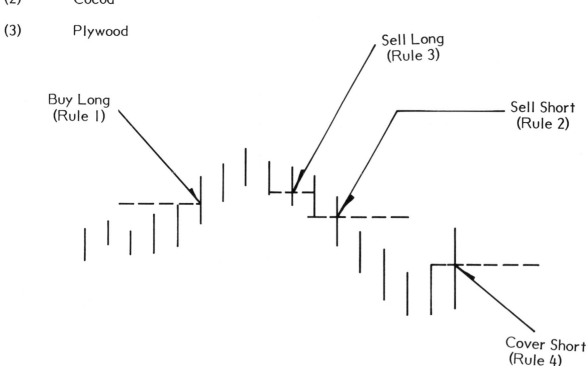

SYSTEM 58

EIGHT WEEK CHANNEL

SYSTEM DEFINITIONS:

(1)   Rule 1:   A Buy signal is generated whenever the price exceeds the high of the previous eight weeks.

(2)   Rule 2:   A Sell signal is generated whenever the price declines below the low of the previous eight weeks.

(3)   When a new Buy or Sell signal is generated, the old position is liquidated simultaneously. In other words, the system is always in the market.

APPLICABLE FOR

(1)   Almost all stocks.

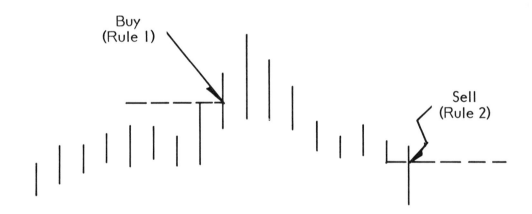

SYSTEM 59

MODIFIED EIGHT WEEK CHANNEL

SYSTEM DEFINITIONS:

(1)   Rule 1:   A Buy signal is generated whenever the price exceeds the high of the previous eight weeks.

(2)   Rule 2:   A Sell signal is generated whenever the price declines below the low of the previous eight weeks.

(3)   Rule 3:   Close out long position, if the price falls below the low of the previous four weeks.

(4)   Rule 4:   Cover your short position, if the price exceeds the high of the previous four weeks.

(5)   The added advantage of the modified system is that it will keep you out of the market some of the time.

APPLICABLE FOR

(1)   Almost all stocks.

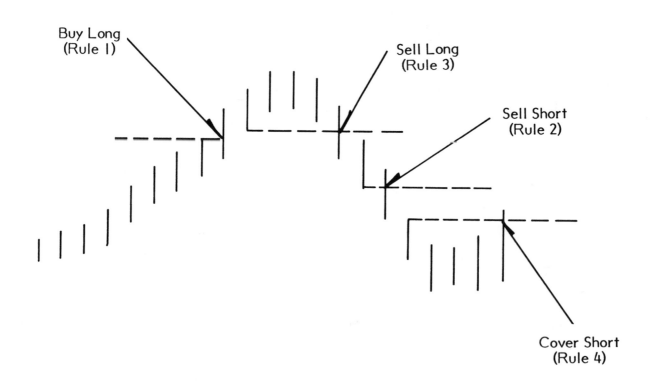

SYSTEM 60

SPEED RESISTANCE LINES

1)   Developed by Edson Gould of Findings and Forecast.

2)   Used extensively by Ike Hasson of the Consultant.

3)   Use a regular bar chart.

4)   Define the top of an uptrend and bottom of downtrend.

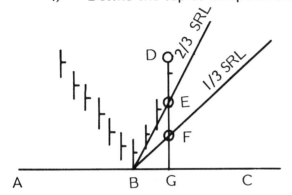 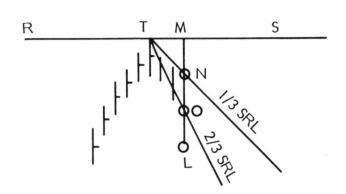

5) (a)   Once the bottom is well defined, draw a line ABCG from the bottom B.

  (b)   Whenever the stock/commodity makes a new high, measure the vertical distance DG between top and bottom.

  (c)   Divide the distance DG in three parts as shown at E and F.

  (d)   Join BE. BE is the 2/3 speed resistance line (SRL).

  (e)   Join BF. BF is the 1/3 speed resistance line (SRL).

  (f)   These lines must be redrawn each time the stock/commodity makes a new high.

  (g)   A strong stock/commodity will stay above its 2/3 SRL.

  (h)   A fairly strong stock/commodity will stay above its 1/3 SRL.

  (i)   When the stock/commodity reacts, the support usually comes around 2/3 SRL.

  (j)   When the stock/commodity penetrates its 2/3 SRL, the next support is at 1/3 SRL.

6) (a)   Once the top is well defined, draw a line RTMS from the top T.

   (b)   Whenever the stock/commodity makes a new low, measure the vertical distance ML.

   (c)   Divide the distance ML in three parts as shown at N and O.

   (d)   Join TO. TO is the 2/3 SRL.

   (e)   Join TN. TN is the 1/3 SRL.

   (f)   A weak stock/commodity will stay below its 2/3 SRL.

   (g)   A fairly weak stock/commodity will stay below its 1/3 SRL.

   (h)   When the weak stock/commodity rallies, the resistance usually comes at 2/3 SRL.

   (i)   When the stock/commodity crosses its 2/3 SRL, the next resistance is at 1/3 SRL.

7)   The system predicts decline in an uptrend and rise in a downtrend.

MODIFIED COLVER METHOD

(L)

A. BAR DEFINITION:

    1.   A key high is a high whose high is preceded and followed by lower daily highs and whose low is preceded and followed by lower daily lows.

        (L) is a key high.

    2.   A key low is defined as the low whose low is preceded and followed by higher daily lows, and whose high is preceded and followed by higher daily highs.

        (M) is a key low.

(M)

B. PHANTOM DEFINITION:

    1.   A key high is a daily high which is preceded and followed by lower daily highs. However, low does not have lower daily lows before and after it.

        (N) is a key high.

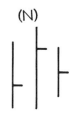

(N)

    2.   A key low is a low which is preceded and followed by higher daily lows. However, high does not have higher daily highs before and after it.

        (O) is a key low.

(O)

C. CLOSE DEFINITION:

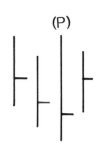

(P)

    1.   A key high is the high whose close is lower than the previous day's close, and is in the lower half of the day's trading range, and whose high is higher than the previous day's high.

        (P) is a key high.

2. A key low is the low whose close is in the upper half of that day's trading range and is higher than the previous day's close, and whose low is lower than the previous day's low.

(Q) is a key low.

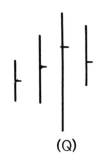

(Q)

D. UNDEFINED

1. Whenever you have two successive key highs without an intervening key low, note the lowest low between the two highs. This will be your key low.

(R) is a key low.

2. Whenever you have two successive key lows without an intervening key high, note the highest high between the two lows. This is your key high.

(S) is a key high.

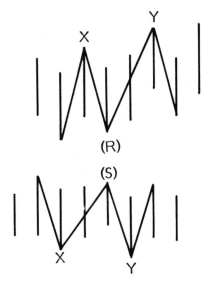

E. Buy signal is generated whenever the commodity/stock rises above a previous key high.

F. Sell signal is generated whenever the commodity/stock falls below a previous key low.

G. Whenever a Buy or Sell signal is generated, the old position is liquidated simultaneously. In other words, the system keeps you in the market all the time.

System 61

MODIFIED COLVER SYSTEM

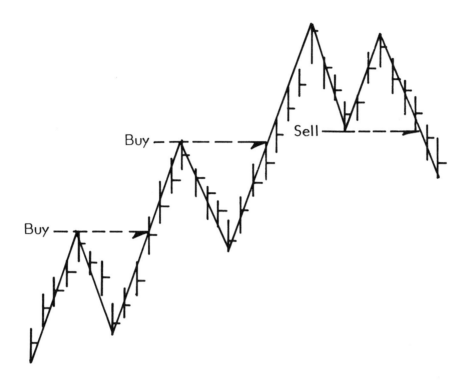

139

SYSTEM 62

MEDIAN LINE METHOD

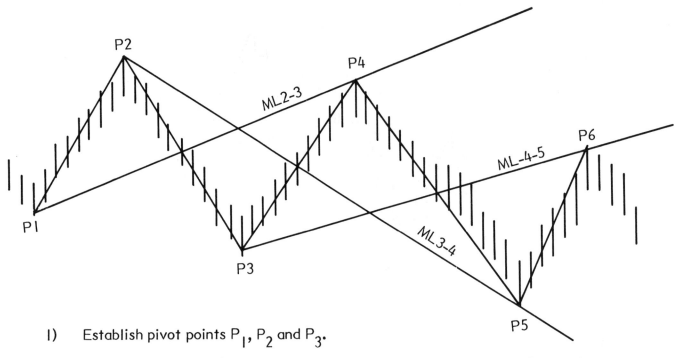

1) Establish pivot points P_1, P_2 and P_3.

2) From pivot point P_1, draw a line bisecting the **distance** between P_2 and P_3. This line is called ML2-3 (median line passing through 2 & 3).

3) This bisecting line ML2-3 is always a test barrier. In other words, the prices will fluctuate around this line.

4) If the prices fail to rise above the test barrier (ML2-3), the rise is finished.

5) This method is like a vector diagram of forces showing the direction of the trend.

6) In advancing market, when the bisectors from the higher and lower pivots point in the upward direction, faster gains can be made trading the long position of the market.

7) In declining market, when the bisectors from the higher and lower pivots point in the downward direction, faster gains can be made trading the short position of the market.

8) When a new pivot P_4 is established, draw a line ML3-4 from P_2 bisecting the distance between P_4 and P_3.

9) This method will tell you in advance the support and resistance levels.

10) Very simple method.

11) Does not require any calculations.

12) Similar to speed resistance lines.

13) Minimizes whip-saws.

14) Closer position to top and bottom pivots is possible.

SYSTEM 63

LAZY LARRY'S EASY METHOD

1) Buy signal is generated if this week's high is above last week's high and this week's close is above the mid-point of this week's range for the second week in a row.

2) Sell signal is generated if this week's low is below last week's low and this week's close is below the mid-point of this week's range for the second week in a row.

3) When a new buy or sell signal is generated, the old position is liquidated simultaneously. In other words, the system always keeps you in the market.

SYSTEM 64

CHART SEGMENT USING TREND LINE

1)   Use regular bar chart showing high, low and close.

2)   Draw the steepest trend line.

3)   Note the closing price after the trend line is broken.

4)   During uptrend, Sell signal is generated when the closing price below the trend line falls below five previous closing prices.

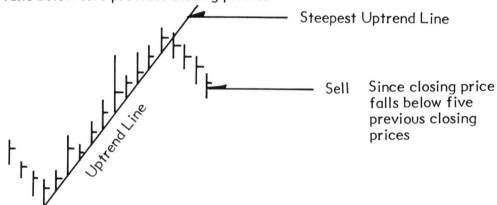

Steepest Uptrend Line

Sell   Since closing price falls below five previous closing prices

5)   During downtrend, Buy signal is generated when the closing price above the trend line rises above five previous closing prices.

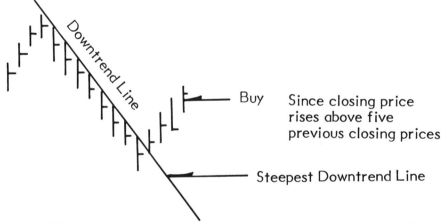

Buy   Since closing price rises above five previous closing prices

Steepest Downtrend Line

6)   When a new Buy or Sell signal is generated, the old position is liquidated simultaneously. In other words, the system always keeps you in the market.

SYSTEM 65

% A METHOD

SYSTEM DEFINITIONS:

1) Col. 1 is the high for today, e.g., 47.00

2) Col. 2 is the low for today, e.g., 44.00

3) Col. 3 is the close for today, e.g., 45.00

4) Col. 4 (5 - D high) is the highest high for the past five days including today.

High	Low	Close	
48.50	47.00	48.00	Day 4
49.50	48.00	48.00	Day 3
46.50	45.00	46.00	Day 2
48.50	46.00	47.25	Day 1
47.00	44.00	45.00	Today

Highest high is 49.50

5) Col. 5 (5 - D low) is the lowest low for the past five days including today.

Lowest low is 44.00

6) Col. 6 (5 - D range) is the difference between Col. 4 and Col. 5

e.g., 49.50 - 44.00 = 5.50

7) Col. 7 (5 - D upward range) is the difference between Col. 4 and Col. 3.

e.g., 49.50 - 45.00 = 4.50

8) $\text{Col. 8} = \dfrac{\text{Col. 7 (5 - D upward range)}}{\text{Col. 6 (5 - D range)}} \times 100\%$. Col. 8 is the %

Alert for the day, e.g., $81.82 = \dfrac{4.50}{5.50} \times 100$

9)   A Buy signal is generated when the % alert is at 90 to 100.

10) A Sell signal is generated when the % alert is at 0 to 10.

11) When a new Buy or Sell signal is generated, the old position is liquidated simultaneously. Thus the system is always in the market.

12) This system should be used with moving average system.

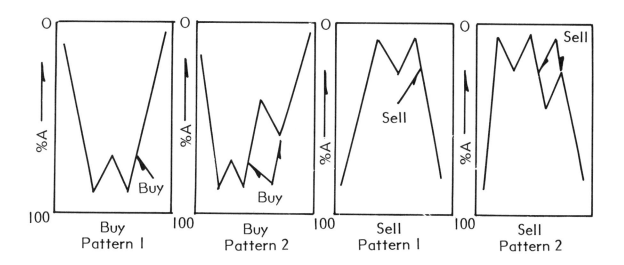

WORK SHEET
SYSTEM 65
% A METHOD

	1 High Price	2 Low Price	3 Close Price	4 (5-D High) Highest High for the past five days	5 (5-D Low) Lowest Low for the past five days	6 (5-D Range) = Col. 4 − Col. 5	7 (5-D Upward range) = Col. 4 − Col. 3	8 (% A) = Col.7 / Col. 6 × 100
1	47.00	44.00	45.00	49.50	44.00	5.50	4.50	81.82
2	49.50	44.00	47.00	49.50	44.00	5.50	2.50	45.45
3	51.50	47.50	50.00	51.50	44.00	7.50	1.50	20.00
4	54.00	51.00	51.00	54.00	44.00	10.00	3.00	30.00
5	55.50	52.00	53.00	55.50	44.00	11.50	2.50	21.74
6	56.00	53.00	54.00	56.00	44.00	12.00	2.00	16.67
7	(57.00)	54.00	56.00	57.00	47.50	9.50	1.00	(10.53)
8	56.00	54.00	55.00	57.00	47.00	11.00	2.00	33.33
9	55.00	53.00	55.00	57.00	44.00	12.00	2.00	16.67
10	54.00	52.50	54.00	57.00	44.00	9.50	3.00	30.00
11	53.00	52.00	53.00	57.00	52.00	5.00	4.00	60.00
12	52.50	(51.00)	51.00	56.00	52.00	5.00	5.00	(100.00)
13	53.00	52.00	52.50	55.00	51.00	4.00	2.50	62.50

Col. 8 annotations: Sell (row with 10.53) · Buy (row with 100.00)

146

SYSTEM 66

% A AND % D METHOD

SYSTEM DEFINITIONS

1) Col. 1 is the high for today, e.g., 47.00

2) Col. 2 is the low for today, e.g., 44.00

3) Col. 3 is the close for today, e.g., 45.00

4) Col. 4 (5 - D high) is the highest high for the past five days including today.

High	Low	Close	
48.50	47.00	48.00	Day 4
49.50	48.00	48.00	Day 3
46.50	45.00	46.00	Day 2
48.50	46.00	47.25	Day 1
47.00	44.00	45.00	Today

Highest high is 49.50

5) Col. 5 (5 - D low) is the lowest low for the past five days including today.

Lowest low is 44.00

6) Col. 6 (5 - D range) is the difference between Col. 4 and Col. 5,

e.g., 49.50 - 44.00 = 5.50

7) Col. 7 (5 - D upward range) is the difference between Col. 4 and Col. 3,

e.g., 49.50 - 45.00 = 4.50

8) $\text{Col. 8} = \dfrac{\text{Col. 7 (5 - D upward range)}}{\text{Col. 6 (5 - D range)}} \times 100\%$. Col. 8 is the %

Alert for the day, e.g., $81.82 = \dfrac{4.50}{5.50} \times 100$

9)   Col. 9 (3 - D moving avg of 5 - D range) is the average of last 3 days of Col. 6.

10)   Col. 10 (3 - D moving avg of 5 - D upward range) is the average of last 3 days of Col. 7.

11)   Col. 11 = $\dfrac{\text{Col. 10 (3 - D Moving Avg of 5 - D upward range)}}{\text{Col. 9 (3 - D Moving Avg of 5 - D range)}}$

      This is % definite.

12)   A Buy signal is generated, when % definite approaches 90 to 95. (% alert will precede % definite by a few days to be an alert for a Buy signal).

13)   A Sell signal is generated, when % definite approaches 0 to 10. (% alert will precede % definite by a few days to be an alert for a Sell signal).

14)   When a new signal is generated, the old position is liquidated.

15)   Use this system with the moving avg system and plot % definite.

16)   Buy and sell patterns are the same as system 65.

WORK SHEET

SYSTEM 66

% A AND % D METHOD

	1 High Price	2 Low Price	3 Close Price	4 (5-D High) Highest High for the past five days	5 (5-D Low) Lowest Low for the past five days	6 (5-D Range) = Col. 4 - Col. 5	7 (5-D Upward Range) = Col. 4 - Col. 3	8 (% A) = Col. 7/Col. 6 × 100	9 3-D Moving Average of 5-D Range	10 3-D Moving Average of 5-D Upward Range	11 (% D) = Col. 10/Col. 9 × 100
1	48.50	47.00	48.00								
2	49.50	48.00	48.00								
3	46.50	45.00	46.00								
4	48.50	46.00	47.25								
5	47.00	44.00	45.00	49.50	44.00	5.50	4.50	81.82			
6	49.50	44.00	47.00	49.50	44.00	5.50	2.50	45.45			
7	51.50	47.50	50.00	51.50	44.00	7.50	1.50	20.00	6.17	2.83	45.87
8	54.00	51.00	51.00	54.00	44.00	10.00	3.00	30.00	7.67	2.33	30.38
9	55.50	52.00	53.00	55.50	44.00	11.50	2.50	21.74	9.67	2.33	24.10
10	56.00	53.00	54.00	56.00	44.00	12.00	2.00	16.67	11.17	2.50	22.38
11	57.00	54.00	56.00	57.00	47.50	9.50	1.00	10.53	11.00	1.83	16.64
12	56.00	54.00	55.00	57.00	51.00	6.00	2.00	33.33	9.17	1.67	18.21
13	55.00	53.00	54.00	57.00	52.00	5.00	3.00	60.00	6.83	2.00	29.28

SYSTEM 67

MOMENTUM TREND INDICATOR I

SYSTEM DEFINITIONS:

1) Col. I is the weekly closing price.

2) Col. 2 is the 5 week exponentially smoothed moving Avg of Col. I.

3) Col. 3 is the 10 week exponentially smoothed moving Avg of Col. I.

4) In Col. 4,   Assign + 2 if the close is above 5 week MA.
   Assign - 2 if the close is above 5 week MA.

5) In Col. 5,   Assign + 3 if the close is above 10 week MA.
   Assign - 3 if the close is below 10 week MA.

6) In Col. 6,   Assign + 2 if the 5 week MA is higher this week than last.
   Assign - 2 if the 5 week MA is lower this week than last.

7) In Col. 7,   Assign + 2 if the 10 week MA is higher this week than last.
   Assign - 2 if the 10 week MA is lower this week than last.

8) In Col. 8,   Assign + I if the 5 week MA is above 10 week MA.
   Assign - I if the 5 week MA is under 10 week MA.

9) Col. 9 =   Momentum Trend Indicator = Col. 4 + Col. 5 + Col. 6 + Col. 7 + Col. 8.

10) Col. 10 is the 5 week moving total of Col. 9.

11) Buy signal is generated when the Col. 10 reaches between 8 to 10, provided Col. 9 does not register - 6 or more.

12) Sell signal is generated when Col. 10 reaches between - 8 to -10, provided Col. 9 does not register + 6 or more.

13) When a new Buy or Sell signal is generated, the old position is liquidated simultaneously. In other words, the system is always in the market.

Strongest signals:	+ 8 to 10 (Col. 10)
Strong signals:	+ 7 (Col. 10)
Fairly strong signals:	+ 5 to 6 (Col. 10)
Medium signals:	+ 4 (Col. 10)
Weak signals:	+ I to 2 (Col. 10)
No signals:	0 (Col. 10)

Market is extremely overbought at	+ 40 to + 50 (Col. 10)
Market is extremely oversold at	- 40 to - 50 (Col. 10)

	1	2	3	4	5	6	7	8	9	10
	Weekly Close Price	5 Week Exponentially Smoothed Moving Avg of Col. 1	10 Week Exponentially Smoothed Moving Avg of Col. 1	Close Above or Below 5 Week MA Above=+2 Below=-2	Close Above or Below 10 Week MA Above=+3 Below=-3	5 Week MA Higher or Lower Higher=+2 Lower=-2	10 Week MA Higher or Lower Higher=+2 Lower=-2	5 Week MA Below or Above 10 Week MA Above=+1 Below=-1	= Col. 4 + Col. 5 + Col. 6 + Col. 7 + Col. 8	5 Week Moving Total of Col. 9
1	49.00	48.40	47.93							
2	50.50	49.09	48.40							
3	51.50	49.89	48.95					—		
4	52.75	50.83	49.64	2	3	2	2	—	10	
5	54.00	51.88	50.42	2	3	2	2	—	10	
6	54.50	52.74	51.16	2	3	2	2	—	10	50
7	56.00	53.82	52.03	2	3	2	2	—	10	50
8	57.50	55.03	53.01	2	3	2	2	—	10	50
9	59.00	56.34	54.09	2	3	2	2	—	10	50
10	60.00	57.55	55.16	2	3	2	2	—	10	50
11	61.50	58.85	56.30	2	3	2	2	—	10	50
12	62.50	60.06	57.41	2	3	2	2	—	10	50
13	63.00	61.03	58.42	2	3	2	2	—	10	50
14	63.50	61.84	59.33	2	3	2	2	—	10	50
15	64.25	62.64	60.22	2	3	2	2	—	10	50
16	63.00	62.76	60.72	2	3	2	2	—	10	50
17	65.00	63.50	61.49	2	3	2	2	—	10	50
18	64.00	63.66	61.94	2	3	2	2	—	10	50

151

SYSTEM 68

MOMENTUM TREND INDICATOR 2

SYSTEM DEFINITIONS:

1)   Col. 1 is the weekly closing price.

2)   Col. 2 is the 5 week exponentially smoothed moving Avg of Col. 1.

3)   Col. 3 is the 10 week exponentially smoothed moving Avg of Col. 1.

4)   Col. 4 is the 15 week exponentially smoothed moving Avg of Col. 1

5)   In Col. 5,   Assign + 1 if the close is above 5 week MA.
                  Assign - 1 if the close is below 5 week MA.

6)   In Col. 6,   Assign + 2 if the close is above 10 week MA.
                  Assign - 2 if the close is below 10 week MA.

7)   In Col. 7,   Assign + 3 if the close is above 15 week MA.
                  Assign - 3 if the close is below 15 week MA.

8)   In Col. 8,   Assign + 1 if the 5 week MA is higher this week than last.
                  Assign - 1 if the 5 week MA is lower this week than last.

9)   In Col. 9,   Assign + 2 if the 10 week MA is higher this week than last.
                  Assign - 2 if the 10 week MA is lower this week than last.

10) In Col. 10, Assign + 3 if the 15 week MA is higher this week than last.
                  Assign - 3 if the 15 week MA is lower this week than last.

11) In Col. 11, Assign + 1 if the 5 week MA is above 10 week MA. Assign - 1
                  if the 5 week MA is below 10 week MA.

12) In Col. 12, Assign + 1 if the 10 week MA is above 15 week MA. Assign - 1
                  if the 10 week MA is below 15 week MA.

13) Col. 13 = Momentum Trend Indicator = Col. 5 + Col. 6 + Col. 7 + Col. 8 +
     Col. 9 + Col. 10 + Col. 11 + Col. 12

14) Col. 14 is the 10 week moving total of Col. 13.

15) Buy signal is generated when Col. 14 reaches between 10 to 12 provided Col.
     13 does not register - 8 or more.

16) Sell signal is generated when Col. 14 reaches between - 10 to - 12 provided
     Col. 13 does not register + 8 or more.

17)   When a new buy or sell signal is generated, the old position is liquidated simultaneously. In other words, the system is always in the market.

Strongest signals: $\pm$ 10 to 12 (Col. 14)
Strong signals: $\pm$ 9 (Col. 14)
Fairly strong signals: $\pm$ 7 to 8 (Col. 14)
Medium signals: $\pm$ 6(Col. 14)
Weak signals: $\pm$ 3 to 4 (Col. 14)
No signals: $\pm$1(Col. 14)

Market is extremely overbought at   + 100 to + 140 (Col. 14)
Market is extremely oversold at   - 100 to - 140 (Col. 14)

WORK SHEET

SYSTEM 68

MOMENTUM TREND INDICATOR 2

	1	2	3	4	5	6	7	8	9	10	11	12	13	14
	Weekly Close Price	5 Week Exponentially Smooth Moving Avg of Col. 1	10 Week Exponentially Smooth Moving Avg of Col. 1	15 Week Exponentially Smooth Moving Avg of Col. 1	Close Above or Below 5 WMA: Above = +1, Below = −1	Close Above or Below 10WMA: Above = +2, Below = −2	Close Above or Below 15WMA: Above = +3, Below = −3	5WMA Up or Down: Up = +1, Down = −1	10WMA Up or Down: Up = +2, Down = −2	15WMA Up or Down: Up = +3, Down = −3	5WMA Above or Below 10WMA: Above = +1, Below = −1	10WMA Above or Below 15WMA: Above = +1, Below = −1	Col. 5+ 6 + 7 + 8 + 9 + 10 + 11 + 12	10 Week Moving Total of Col. 13
1	49.00	48.40	47.93	47.33	1	2	3	1	2	3	1	1	14	
2	50.50	49.09	48.40	47.74	1	2	3	1	2	3	1	1	14	
3	51.50	49.89	48.95	48.23	1	2	3	1	2	3	1	1	14	
4	52.75	50.83	49.64	48.82	1	2	3	1	2	3	1	1	14	
5	54.00	51.88	50.42	49.49	1	2	3	1	2	3	1	1	14	
6	54.50	52.74	51.16	50.14	1	2	3	1	2	3	1	1	14	
7	56.00	53.82	52.03	50.90	1	2	3	1	2	3	1	1	14	
8	57.50	55.03	53.01	51.76	1	2	3	1	2	3	1	1	14	
9	59.00	56.34	54.09	52.70	1	2	3	1	2	3	1	1	14	
10	60.00	57.55	55.16	53.65	1	2	3	1	2	3	1	1	14	140
11	61.50	58.85	56.30	54.67	1	2	3	1	2	3	1	1	14	140
12	52.50	60.06	57.41	55.69	1	2	3	1	2	3	1	1	14	140
13	63.00	61.03	58.42	56.64	1	2	3	1	2	3	1	1	14	140
14	63.50	61.84	59.33	57.53	1	2	3	1	2	3	1	1	14	140
15	64.25	62.64	60.22	58.40	1	2	3	1	2	3	1	1	14	140
16	63.00	62.76	60.72	59.00	1	2	3	1	2	3	1	1	14	140
17	65.00	63.50	61.49	59.78	1	2	3	1	2	3	1	1	14	140
18	64.00	63.66	61.94	60.33	1	2	3	1	2	3	1	1	14	140

154

SYSTEM 69

MOMENTUM TREND INDICATOR 3

System Definitions:

1) Col. 1 is the weekly closing price.

2) Col. 2 is the 3 week exponentially smoothed moving avg of Col. 1.

3) Col. 3 = RCI = $\dfrac{\text{3 week MA this week - 3 week MA one week ago}}{\text{3 week MA one week ago}}$

4) Col. 4 = $\dfrac{\text{Closing Price - 3 week MA}}{\text{3 week MA}}$

5) Col. 5 = Momentum Trend Indicator = Col. 3 + Col. 4.

6) Col. 6 is the five week exponentially smoothed moving avg of Col. 5.

7) Sell signal is generated when the oscillator tops-out (successive higher readings followed by a lower reading) provided the oscillator reversal point is in the positive territory, e.g., 1.20, 1.30, 1.35, 1.40, 1.25.

8) Buy signal is generated when the oscillator bottoms-out (successive lower readings followed by a higher reading) provided the oscillator reversal point is in the negative territory, e.g., -1.20, -1.30, -1.40, -1.10.

9) When a new Buy or Sell signal is generated, the old position is liquidated simultaneously. In other words, the system is always in the market.

155

WORK SHEET

SYSTEM 69

MOMENTUM TREND INDICATOR 3

	1 Weekly Close Price	2 3 week Exponent- ially smoothed Moving Avg of Col. 1	3 RC 1 based on Col.2	4 = Col.1−Col.2 Col.2	5 = Col.3 + Col.4	6 5 Week Exponent- ially smoothed Moving Avg of Col. 5	
1	37.50	37.08	1.37	1.13	2.50		
2	38.08	37.61	1.43	1.25	2.68		
3	37.17	37.58	− .08	−1.09	−1.17		
4	39.00	38.29	1.89	1.85	3.74		
5	36.75	37.52	−2.01	−2.05	−4.06	0.74	
6	35.13	36.33	−3.17	−3.30	−6.47	−1.64	Bottom
7	(36.00)	36.16	− .47	− .44	−0.91	(−1.40)	Buy
8	36.25	36.21	0.14	0.11	0.25	−.85	
9	35.75	35.98	−.72	−.64	−1.36	1.02	
10	35.75	35.86	− .33	−.31	− .64	− .90	
11	37.75	36.81	2.65	2.55	5.20	1.12	
12	38.25	37.53	1.96	1.92	3.88	2.03	Top
13	(35.00)	36.26	−3.38	−3.47	−6.85	(− .90)	Sell
14	35.50	35.88	−1.05	−1.06	−2.11	−1.30	
15	35.00	35.44	−1.23	−1.24	−2.47	−1.69	Bottom
16	(36.38)	35.91	1.33	1.31	2.64	(−.26)	Buy
17	36.50	36.21	0.84	0.80	1.64	0.37	Top
18	(36.25)	36.23	0.06	0.06	0.12	(0.29)	Sell
19	36.75	36.49	0.72	0.71	1.43	0.66	
20	36.00	36.24	− .69	− .66	−1.35	−.0009	
21	35.00	35.62	−1.71	−1.74	−3.45	−1.14	
22	34.50	35.06	−1.57	−1.60	−3.17	−1.81	
23	32.75	33.91	−3.28	−3.42	−6.70	−3.42	Bottom
24	(33.00)	33.45	−1.36	−1.35	−2.71	(−3.19)	Buy
25	34.25	33.85	1.20	1.18	2.38	−1.35	
26	34.50	34.18	0.97	0.94	1.91	− .27	
27	35.25	34.71	1.55	1.56	3.11	0.84	
28	36.75	35.73	2.94	2.85	5.79	2.48	Top
29	(35.25)	35.49	− .67	− .68	−1.35	(1.21)	Sell

SYSTEM 70

MOMENTUM TREND INDICATOR 4

SYSTEM DEFINITIONS:

1)   Col. 1 is the weekly closing price.

2)   Col. 2 is the 3 week exponentially smoothed moving avg of Col. 1.

3)   Col. 3 is the 6 week exponentially smoothed moving avg of Col. 1.

4)   Col. 4 = RCI = $\dfrac{\text{3 week MA this week - 3 week MA one week ago}}{\text{3 week MA one week ago}}$

5)   Col. 5 = RCI = $\dfrac{\text{6 week MA this week - 6 week MA one week ago}}{\text{6 week MA one week ago}}$

6)   Col. 6 = $\dfrac{\text{Closing price - 3 week MA}}{\text{3 week MA}}$

7)   Col. 7 = $\dfrac{\text{Closing price - 6 week MA}}{\text{6 week MA}}$

8)   Col. 8 = Momentum Trend Indicator = Col. 4 + Col. 5 + Col. 6 + Col. 7

9)   Sell signal is generated when the oscillator tops-out (Successive higher readings followed by a lower reading) provided the oscillator reversal point is in the positive territory, e.g., 1.20, 1.25, 1.30, 1.35, 1.40, 1.37.

10) Buy signal is generated when the oscillator bottoms-out (successive lower readings followed by a higher reading) provided the oscillator reversal point is in the negative territory, e.g., -1.20, -1.30, -1.40, -1.20.

11) When a new Buy or Sell signal is generated, the old position is liquidated simultaneously. In other words, the system is always in the market.

WORK SHEET

SYSTEM 70

MOMENTUM TREND INDICATOR 4

	1	2	3	4	5	6	7	8	
	Weekly Close Price	3 Week Expn smoothed Moving Avg of Col. 1	6 Week Expn Smoothed Moving Avg of Col. 1	RC 1 based on Col. 2	RC 1 based on Col.3	= Col.1−Col.2 / Col.2	= Col.1−Col.3 / Col.3	= Col.4 + Col.5 + Col.6 + Col.7	
1	39.00	38.29	37.64		1.51	1.85	3.61	8.86	
2	36.75	37.52	37.38	1.89	−.69	−2.05	−1.69	−6.44	
3	35.13	36.33	36.73	−2.01	−1.74	−3.30	−4.36	−12.57	Bottom
4	36.00	36.16	36.52	−3.17	−.57	−.44	−1.42	−2.90	Buy
5	36.25	36.21	36.44	−.47	−.22	0.11	−.52	−.49	
6	35.75	35.88	36.24	0.14	−.55	−.64	−1.35	−3.26	
7	35.75	35.86	36.10	−.72	−.39	−.31	−.97	−2.00	
8	37.75	36.81	36.58	−.33	1.33	2.55	3.20	9.73	Top
9	38.25	37.53	37.06	2.65	1.31	1.92	3.21	8.40	Sell
10	35.00	36.26	36.46	1.96	−1.62	−3.47	−4.00	−12.47	Bottom
11	35.50	35.88	36.19	−3.38	−.74	−1.06	−1.91	−4.76	Buy
12	35.00	35.44	35.84	−1.05	−.97	−1.24	−2.34	−5.78	
13	36.38	35.91	36.00	−1.23	0.45	1.31	1.06	4.15	Top
14	36.50	36.21	36.14	1.33	0.39	0.80	1.00	3.03	Sell
15	36.25	36.23	36.17	0.84	0.08	0.06	0.22	0.42	
16	36.75	36.49	36.34	0.06	0.47	0.71	1.13	3.03	
17	36.00	36.24	36.24	0.72	.28	−.66	−.66	−2.29	
18	35.00	35.62	35.88	−.69	−.99	−1.74	−2.45	−6.89	
19	34.50	35.06	35.48	−1.71	−1.11	−1.60	−2.76	−7.04	
20	32.75	33.91	34.69	−1.57	−2.23	−3.42	−5.59	−14.52	Bottom
21	33.00	33.45	34.20	−3.28	−1.41	−1.35	−3.51	−7.63	Buy
22	34.25	33.85	34.21	−1.36	.03	1.18	0.12	2.53	
23	34.50	34.18	34.30	1.20	0.26	0.94	0.58	2.75	
24	35.25	34.71	34.57	0.97	0.79	1.56	1.97	5.87	
25	36.75	35.73	35.20	2.94	1.82	2.85	4.40	12.01	Top
26	35.25	35.49	35.22	−.67	0.06	−.68	0.09	−1.20	Sell

SYSTEM 71

MOMENTUM TREND INDICATOR 5

SYSTEM DEFINITIONS:

1)   Col. 1 is the weekly closing price.

2)   Col. 2 is the 5 week exponentially smoothed moving avg of Col. 1.

3)   Col. 3 is the 10 week exponentially smoothed moving avg of Col. 1.

4)   Col. 4 is the 15 week exponentially smoothed moving avg of Col. 1.

5)   Col. 5 = RCI = $\dfrac{\text{5 week MA this week - 5 week MA 1 week ago}}{\text{5 week MA 1 week ago}}$

6)   Col. 6 = RCI = $\dfrac{\text{10 week MA this week - 10 week MA 1 week ago}}{\text{10 week MA 1 week ago}}$

7)   Col. 7 = RCI = $\dfrac{\text{15 week MA this week - 15 week MA 1 week ago}}{\text{15 week MA 1 week ago}}$

8)   Col. 8 = $\dfrac{\text{Closing price - 5 week MA}}{\text{5 week MA}}$

9)   Col. 9 = $\dfrac{\text{Closing price - 10 week MA}}{\text{10 week MA}}$

10)   Col. 10 = $\dfrac{\text{Closing price - 15 week MA}}{\text{15 week MA}}$

11)   Col. 11 = Momentum Trend Indicator = Col. 5 + Col. 6 + Col. 7 + Col. 8 + Col. 9 + Col. 10

12)   Col. 12 is the 7 week exponentially smoothed moving avg of Col. 11.

13)   Sell signal is generated when the top reversal point in Col. 12 declines by 7%, e.g., 28.93 x (1-.07) = 26.90.

14)   Buy signal is generated when the bottom reversal point in Col. 12 exceeds by 7%.

15)   When a new Buy or Sell signal is generated, the old position is liquidated simultaneously. In other words, the system is always in the market.

WORK SHEET

SYSTEM 71

MOMENTUM TREND INDICATOR 5

	1 — Weekly Close Price	2 — 5 Week Expn smooth moving Avg of Col.1	3 — 10 Week Expn smooth moving Avg of Col.1	4 — 15 Week Expn smooth moving Avg of Col.1	5 — RC 1 based on Col.2	6 — RC 1 based on Col.3	7 — RC 1 based on Col.4	8 — $\frac{1-2}{2}=$	9 — $\frac{1-3}{3}=$	10 — $\frac{1-4}{4}=$	11 — Col.5 + Col.6 + Col.7 + Col.8 + Col.9 + Col.10 =	12 — 7 Week Expn smooth moving Avg of Col.11	
1	49.00	48.40	47.93	47.33									
2	50.50	49.09	48.40	47.74	1.43	0.98	0.87	2.87	4.34	5.78	16.27		
3	51.50	49.89	48.95	48.23	1.63	1.14	1.03	3.23	5.21	6.78	19.02		
4	52.75	50.83	49.64	48.82	1.88	1.41	1.22	3.78	6.27	8.05	22.61		
5	54.00	51.88	50.42	49.49	2.07	1.57	1.37	4.09	7.10	9.11	25.31		
6	54.50	52.74	51.16	50.14	1.66	1.47	1.31	3.34	6.53	8.70	23.01		
7	56.00	53.82	52.03	50.90	2.05	1.70	1.52	4.05	7.63	10.02	26.97		
8	57.50	55.03	53.01	51.76	2.25	1.88	1.69	4.49	8.47	11.09	29.87		
9	59.00	56.34	54.09	52.70	2.38	2.04	1.82	4.72	9.08	11.95	31.99	23.29	
10	60.00	57.55	55.16	53.65	2.15	1.98	1.80	4.26	8.77	11.84	30.80	25.47	
11	61.50	58.85	56.30	54.67	2.26	2.07	1.90	4.50	9.24	12.49	32.46	26.80	
12	62.50	60.06	57.41	55.69	2.06	1.97	1.87	4.06	8.87	12.23	31.06	28.21	Top
13	63.00	61.03	58.42	56.64	1.62	1.76	1.71	3.23	7.84	11.23	27.39	28.54	
14	63.50	61.84	59.33	57.53	1.33	1.56	1.57	2.68	7.03	10.38	24.55	27.54	
15	(64.25)	62.64	60.22	58.40	1.29	1.50	1.51	2.57	6.69	10.02	23.58	(26.55)	Sell
16	63.00	62.76	60.72	59.00	0.19	0.83	1.03	0.38	3.75	6.78	12.96	23.15	
17	65.00	63.50	61.49	59.78	1.18	1.27	1.32	2.36	5.71	8.73	20.57	22.51	
18	64.00	63.66	61.94	60.33	0.25	0.73	0.92	0.53	3.33	6.08	11.84	19.84	

SYSTEM 72

MOMENTUM TREND INDICATOR 6

SYSTEM DEFINITIONS:

1)   Col. I is the weekly closing price.

2)   Col. 2 = RC5 = $\dfrac{\text{Closing price this week - closing price 5 weeks ago}}{\text{Closing price 5 weeks ago}}$

3)   Col. 3 is the 5 week exponentially smoothed moving average of Col. 2.

4)   Buy signal is generated, when

    a)   The amount of decline in Col. 3 has diminished to a level less than -1% (or become positive) and

    b)   The current rate of change in Col. 2 has already turned into a positive number.

5)   Sell signal is generated, when

    a)   The amount of increase in Col. 3 has diminished to a level less than +1% (or become negative) and

    b)   The current rate of change in Col. 2 has already turned into a negative number.

6)   When a new Buy or Sell signal is generated, the old position is liquidated simultaneously. In other words, the system is always in the market.

7)   Completely mechanical method.

WORK SHEET

SYSTEM 72

MOMENTUM TREND INDICATOR 6

	1	2	3	
	Weekly Close Price	RC 5 Based on Col.1	5 Week Exponentially smoothed moving Avg. of Col. 2	
1	63.50			
2	63.00			
3	62.50			
4	63.00			
5	62.50			
6	62.63	-1.37		
7	63.50	0.79		
8	64.75	3.60		
9	64.75	2.78		
10	64.75	3.60	1.88	
11	65.50	4.58	2.77	
12	66.00	3.94	3.16	
13	66.50	2.70	3.01	
14	66.25	2.32	2.78	
15	66.50	2.70	2.75	
16	67.50	3.05	2.85	
17	67.75	2.65	2.78	
18	68.00	2.26	2.61	
19	67.75	2.26	2.50	
20	67.25	1.13	2.04	
21	66.50	-1.48	.88	Sell
22	64.50	-4.80	-.98	
23	62.50	-8.09	-3.33	
24	61.50	-9.23	-5.28	
25	59.50	-11.52	-7.34	
26	58.50	-12.03	-8.89	
27	58.50	-9.30	-9.02	
28	59.50	-4.80	-7.63	
29	60.50	-1.63	-5.65	
30	61.50	3.36	-2.68	
31	62.00	5.98	0.18	Buy
32	62.50	6.84	2.38	

SYSTEM 73

FILTERING

THEORY AND DISCUSSION:

(1)   The trend for commodity is up if the current closing price is above its closing price 5 weeks ago.

(2)   The trend for commodity is down if the current closing price is below its closing price 5 weeks ago.

(3)   The trend for stock is up if the current closing price is above its closing price 10 weeks ago.

(4)   The trend for stock is down if the current closing price is below its closing price 10 weeks ago.

SYSTEM DEFINITIONS:

(1)   Col. 1 is the high price.

(2)   Col. 2 is the low price.

(3)   Col. 3 is the close price.

(4)   Determine the trend by above definitions.

(5)   If the trend is up, note the new high with circle, e.g.,52.00, 52.50, 53.00

(6)   If the trend is down, note the new low with square, e.g.,50.00, 49.00, 48.00.

(7)   Use the following filters.

   8% for below $20
   7% for $20 to $39
   6% for $40 to $59
   5% for $60 to $199
   4% for over $199

(8)   Since the stock under consideration is between 20 and 40, we will use 7% filter.

163

(9) For uptrend, the downward reversal signal is obtained by multiplying the highest high price by (1-.07), e.g.,37 x .93 = 34.41.

(10) For downtrend, the upward reversal signal is obtained by multiplying the lowest low price by (1 + .07), e.g.,34 x 1.07 = 36.38.

(11) Sell signal is generated when the current low price falls below the downward reversal signal for uptrend.

(12) Buy signal is generated when the current high price exceeds the upward reversal signal for downtrend.

(13) When a new Buy or Sell signal is generated, the old position is liquidated simultaneously. In other words, the system is always in the market.

WORK SHEET

SYSTEM 73

FILTERING

	1	2	3	4	5	
	High Price	Low Price	Close Price	Downward Reversal signal for uptrend	Upward Reversal signal for Downtrend	
1	35.00	34.00	34.50			The Trend is up.
2	36.00	35.50	35.75			
3	36.75	35.75	36.00	34.35		
4	37.00	36.50	36.75	34.58		
5	37.00	36.00	36.50	34.58		
6	37.75	36.00	36.50	35.28		
7	38.00	36.00	37.00	35.51		
8	39.00	36.75	37.00	36.45		
9	38.75	37.00	37.50	36.45		
10	38.50	37.00	37.63	36.45		
11	37.00	36.00	36.25	36.45		Since the Low
12	36.00	35.00	35.50		37.45	drops below 36.45
13	35.75	34.00	34.50		36.38	(Downward reversal
14	35.00	34.00	34.50		36.38	signal), we Sell
15	34.00	33.00	33.50		35.31	at 36.00.
16	33.50	32.75	33.00		35.04	
17	33.00	32.00	32.50		34.24	
18	33.50	32.50	33.00		34.24	
19	34.00	32.50	33.50		34.24	
20	34.50	33.00	34.00		34.24	Since the high rises above 34.24 (upward reversal signal), we Buy at 34.50.

SYSTEM 74

SWING INDEX

THEORY AND DISCUSSION:

(1)   The trend for commodity is up if the current closing price is above its closing price 5 weeks ago.

(2)   The trend for commodity is down if the current closing price is below its closing price 5 weeks ago.

(3)   The trend for stock is up if the current closing price is above its closing price 10 weeks ago.

(4)   The trend for stock is down if the current closing price is below its closing price 10 weeks ago.

SYSTEM DEFINITIONS:

(1)   Col. 1 is the high price.

(2)   Col. 2 is the low price.

(3)   Col. 3 is the close price.

(4)   Determine the trend by above definitions.

(5)   If the trend is up, note the new high with circle, e.g.,52.00,⟨53.00⟩

(6)   If the trend is down, note the new low with square, e.g.,49.00, ☐48.00.☐

(7)   Use the following filters.

  5% for below $20
  4% for $20 to $39
  3% for $40 to $59
  2% for $60 to $199
  1 1/2% for over $200

(8)   Since the stock is $100, we will use 2% filter.

(9)   For uptrend, the downward reversal signal is obtained by multiplying the highest high price by (1-.02), e.g.,100 x .98 = 98.00.

(10)   For downtrend, the upward reversal signal is obtained by multiplying the lowest low price by (1+.02), e.g.,100 x 1.02 = 102.00.

(11)   Downward reversal is generated, when the current low price falls below the downward reversal signal for uptrend.

(12)   Upward reversal is generated, when the current high price exceeds the upward reversal signal for downtrend.

(13)   Buy signal is generated, when the last high is exceeded on the upside.

(14)   Sell signal is generated, when the last low is penetrated on the downside.

(15)   When a new Buy or Sell signal is generated, the old position is liquidated simultaneously. In other words, the system is always in the market.

166

WORK SHEET

SYSTEM 74

SWING INDEX

	1	2	3	4	5	
	High Price	Low Price	Close Price	Downward Reversal signal for uptrend	Upward Reversal signal for Downtrend	
1	100.00	99.00	99.50			The trend is up
2	101.00	99.50	100.00	99.02		
3	102.00	101.00	101.50	100.00		
4	103.05	101.50	102.00	101.03		Downward reversal from 103.05 (1)
5	101.50	100.00	101.00	101.03		
6	101.75	101.00	101.50		102.00	
7	100.50	99.00	100.00		100.98	
8	100.75	99.50	99.50		100.98	
9	100.00	99.00	99.50		100.98	Upward reversal from 99.00 (2)
10	101.00	100.00	100.50		100.98	
11	103.00	102.00	102.50	100.98		
12	104.00	103.00	103.50	101.96		
13	105.00	104.00	105.00	102.94		
14	107.00	106.00	107.00	104.90		
15	109.00	108.00	108.50	106.86		
16	112.00	111.00	112.00	109.80		Downward reversal from 112.00 (3)
17	111.00	109.00	110.00	109.80		
18	110.00	109.00	109.00		111.18	
19	110.00	109.00	109.50		111.18	Upward reversal from 109.00 (4)
20	112.00	110.00	110.50		111.18	Downward reversal from 112.00 (5)
21	111.00	110.00	110.00	109.80		
22	110.00	109.00	109.00	109.80		
23	109.00	108.00	108.00		110.16	
24	107.00	106.00	106.50		108.12	
25	106.00	104.00	105.00		106.08	

SWING INDEX

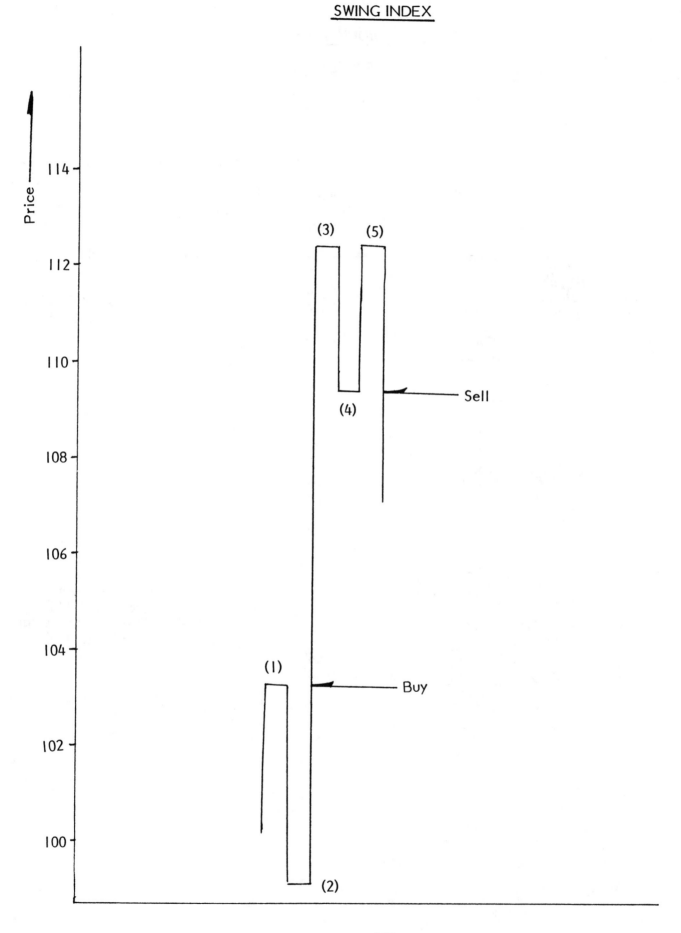

SYSTEM 75

MODIFIED ENGINEER'S METHOD

GENERAL THEORY AND DISCUSSION:

(1)   Circle the low which you think is a low.

(2)   Circle the high which you think is a high.

(3)   After a low is made, wait for at least four days including a low day before you test any plus factors.

(4)   If a new low is made during these four days, count another four days from this new low including new low before testing any plus factors.

(5)   After a high is made, wait for at least four days including a high day before testing any minus factors.

(6)   If a new high is made during these four days, count another four days from this new high including new high before testing any minus factors.

7) <u>Plus Factor:</u>   Three higher closes during four or more days - no new low made.

H	L	C
46.00	45.00	45.50
45.00	(44.00)	44.50
44.75	44.25	44.50
44.85	44.50	(44.75)
45.00	44.75	(44.85)

Three higher closes are made as circled above. This satisfies plus factor.

H	L	C
57.00	55.75	56.00
56.50	(55.00)	55.75
56.75	55.25	(56.85)
57.00	55.28	55.75
56.85	55.00	55.65

Only two higher closes as circled above are made. This doesn't satisfy plus factor.

H	L	C
75.25	74.00	74.50
75.00	(74.00)	(74.00)
75.50	74.25	74.50
75.35	(74.00)	(74.60)
75.00	(73.75)	(74.50)

Three higher closes are made but a new low is made within these four days. This doesn't satisfy plus factor.

H	L	C
65.00	(64.00)	64.50
65.00	64.25	(64.75)
64.75	64.15	(64.50)
64.85	64.18	(64.60)
64.95	64.28	64.65
65.00	64.50	(64.85)

Three higher closes over a period of six days are made. No new low is made. Therefore, this satisfies plus factor.

8) <u>Plus Factor:</u>   Close above any three previous highs during four or more days.

H	L	C
(56.75)	56.00	56.25
(56.85)	56.25	56.75
(56.95)	56.50	56.95
(57.00)	56.00	(57.00)

Satisfies

H	L	C
(45.50)	45.00	45.25
45.75	45.25	45.50
45.85	45.50	45.65
45.95	45.50	(45.75)

Doesn't Satisfy

H	L	C
(75.50)	75.00	75.00
(75.65)	75.50	75.50
75.85	74.75	75.65
75.00	74.85	(75.75)

Doesn't Satisfy

H	L	C
(65.00)	64.00	64.50
(65.15)	64.25	64.75
(65.25)	64.50	65.00
66.00	65.00	65.25
66.50	65.50	(65.75)

Satisfies

(9) Plus Factor: <u>Low above any three previous highs during four or more days.</u>

H	L	C		H	L	C
(46.00)	45.00	45.50		(46.00)	45.00	45.50
(46.75)	46.00	46.25		46.00	45.25	45.50
(46.95)	46.50	46.95		(46.75)	46.00	46.25
47.25	(47.00)	47.25		(46.95)	46.50	46.95
				47.25	(47.00)	47.25

Satisfies   Satisfies

H	L	C		H	L	C
(56.00)	55.00	55.75		(56.00)	55.00	55.75
(56.25)	55.25	55.50		(56.25)	55.25	55.50
56.75	56.00	56.25		56.50	56.00	56.25
57.00	(56.50)	56.75		57.00	(56.50)	56.75

Doesn't Satisfy   Doesn't Satisfy

(10) Plus Factor:

Close above any three previous closes during four or more days.

<u>Low above any three previous lows during four or more days.</u>

<u>High above any three previous highs during four or more days.</u>

H	L	C		H	L	C
(46.00)	(45.00)	(45.50)		(46.00)	(45.00)	(45.50)
(46.25)	(45.25)	(45.60)		(46.00)	(45.00)	(45.50)
(46.50)	(45.50)	(45.75)		(46.25)	(45.25)	(45.60)
(46.75)	(45.75)	(46.00)		(46.50)	(45.50)	(45.75)
				(46.75)	(45.75)	(46.00)

Satisfies   Satisfies

H	L	C		H	L	C
(46.00)	(45.00)	(45.50)		(46.00)	(45.00)	(45.50)
(46.25)	(45.25)	(45.60)		(46.25)	(45.25)	(45.60)
(46.50)	(45.50)	(45.75)		(46.50)	(45.50)	(45.75)
(46.75)	(45.50)	(46.00)		(46.75)	(45.75)	(46.00)

Doesn't Satisfy   Doesn't Satisfy

(11) Plus Factor:

Close above most recent three (3) previous highs during four or more days.

Same as Item 8 but instead of using any three previous highs, use the most recent three highs.

(12) Minus factors work in the same way as plus factors, but in the opposite direction.

SYSTEM DEFINITIONS:

(1) Put High Price in Col. 1.

(2) Put Low Price in Col. 2.

(3) Put Close Price in Col. 3.

(4) Put 5 Day Average of Closes in Col. 4.

(5) Run up = $\dfrac{\text{High Today} + \text{Low yesterday} + \text{close the day before yesterday}}{3}$

Put Run up in Col. 5.

(6) Run Down = $\dfrac{\text{Close Today} + \text{Low Yesterday} + \text{High the day before yesterday}}{3}$

Put run down in Col. 6.

Plus Factors (from a low day including low day)

(7) Assign 1 for three higher closes during four or more days-no new low made. (Col. 7)

(8) Assign 1 for close above any three previous highs during four or more days. (Col. 8)

(9) Assign 1 for close above 5 day close average. (Col. 9)

(10) Assign 1 for close above Run Down. (Col. 10)

(11) Assign 1 for Low above any three previous highs during four days or more. (Col. 11)

(12)   Assign 1 for close above any three previous closes (during four or more days) and low above any three previous lows (during four or more days), and high above any three previous highs (during four or more days). (Col. 12)

(13)   Assign 1 for close above most recent three previous highs during four or more days. (Col. 13)

(14)   Assign 0 if none of the above plus factors are met.

Minus Factors (from a high day including high day)

(15)   Assign -1 for three lower closes during four or more days-no new high made. (Col.7)

(16)   Assign -1 for close below any three previous lows during four or more days. (Col.8)

(17)   Assign -1 for close below 5 day close average. (Col. 9)

(18)   Assign -1 for close below Run up. (Col. 10)

(19)   Assign -1 for high below any three previous lows during four or more days. (Col.11)

(20)   Assign -1 for close below any three previous closes (during four or more days) and high below any three previous highs (during four or more days) and low below any three previous lows (during four or more days). (Col. 12)

(21)   Assign -1 for close below most recent three previous lows during four or more days. (Col.13)

(22)   Assign 0 if none of the above minus factors are met.

(23)   A Buy signal is generated for 6 or more points.

(24)   A sell signal is generated for -6 or more points.

(25)   When a new Buy or Sell signal is generated, the old position is liquidated simultaneously. In other words, the system is always in the market.

MODIFIED ENGINEER'S METHOD

	1	2	3	4	5	6	7	8	9	10	11	12	13	
	High Price	Low Price	Close Price	5 Day Close Average	Run Up	Run Down								Number of points
1	53.75	52.75	53.00											
2	53.50	52.65	52.95											
3	53.25	52.55	52.85											
4	53.00	52.25	52.75											
5	53.25	52.35	53.00											
6	53.50	52.50	53.25											
7	54.00	53.75	53.85	53.14		53.25	1	1	1	1	1	1	1	7 Buy
8	54.63	54.00	54.25											
9	55.00	54.50	54.75											
10	55.75	55.00	55.25											
11	56.00	55.50	55.75											
12	56.50	56.00	56.25											
13	57.00	56.50	56.75											
14	58.00	56.50	56.75		56.50									
15	58.50	56.75	57.00		56.33		-1	-1	-1	-1	-1	-1	-1	-7 Sell
16	58.00	56.50	56.75											
17	57.00	56.25	56.50											
18	56.00	55.00	55.50											
19	55.50	54.75	55.25											
20	55.00	54.50	55.00											
21	54.75	54.25	54.50											

Notes:
(1) Calculate 5 Day Average only when necessary.
(2) Calculate only Run Down when testing Bottom.
(3) Calculate only Run Up when testing Top.

SYSTEM 76

ONLY FOR STOCK OPTION TRADERS

This system is basically the same as system 75 (Modified Engineer's Method). Instead of using daily High, Low and Close, we will use High, Low and Close based on three days as explained below.

Daily Basis			Three Day Basis		
High	Low	Close	High	Low	Close
53.50	52.75	53.00			
53.25	52.00	53.00			
53.00	52.25	52.50	53.50	52.00	52.50
53.00	52.35	52.75			
53.50	53.00	53.25			
54.00	53.25	53.75	54.00	52.35	53.75
54.63	53.50	54.38			
55.50	54.00	54.25			
56.38	55.50	55.75	56.38	53.50	55.75

SYSTEM 77

SIGMA SYSTEM

GENERAL THEORY AND DISCUSSION:

(1)   The trends started from a large counter trend movement tend to persist.

(2)   This calculation yields the value of the size of the counter trend move.

(3)   This is a method of constantly optimizing point and figure charts or constantly optimizing price filters.

(4)   Since the stock under consideration is between 20 and 40, we will use 7% price filter as discussed in system 6.

        Downward Price Reversal Distance = Highest close x .07
$$= 39.50 \times .07$$
$$= 2.76$$
In other words, we will reverse our position whenever there is a change of 2.76 from the highest close.

(5)   For our example, Downward price reversal distance as calculated by Sigma System is 1.54.

(6)   Use past data for at least two or three months for calculating σ.

SYSTEM DEFINITIONS:

(1)   Col. 1 is the closing price.

(2)   Col. 2 is the price change (compared to previous price).

(3)   Col. 3 is the size change. Start with smallest ($\pm$) price change and go to the largest ($\pm$) price change, e.g, +1/8, -1/8, -1/4, +1/2, -1/2, +3/4, +1 and +1 1/2. Denote Col. 3 by C.

(4)   Col. 4 is the number of cases, e.g.,Count how many times price changed by +1/8 and put this number in Col. 4. In our problem +1/8 changed three times; so we will put 3 in Col. 4. Denote Col. 4 by g.

(5)   Col. 5, denoted by n, is the accumulation of Col. 4.

(6)   Col. 6 is $C^2 = (\text{Col. 3})^2$

(7)   Col. 7 $= gC^2 = $ Col. 4 x Col. 6

(8)   Col. 8 is ΣgC^2. i.e. add all values in Col. 7 and put in Col. 8.

(9)   Col. 9 is $\Sigma gC^2/_n = \dfrac{\text{Col. 8}}{\text{Col. 5}}$

(10) Col. 10 is $\sqrt{\Sigma gC^2/_n} = \sqrt{\text{Col. 9}}$

(11) Col. 11 $= 2\sqrt{\dfrac{\Sigma gC^2}{n}} = 2 \times$ Col. 10

WORK SHEET

SYSTEM 77

SIGMA SYSTEM

	1	2	3	4	5	6	7	8	9	10	11
	Closing Price	Price Change	Size Change	No. of Cases	Accumulation of Col.4	C^2	gC^2	ΣgC^2	$\dfrac{\Sigma gC^2}{n}$	$\sqrt{\dfrac{\Sigma gC^2}{n}}$	$2\sqrt{\dfrac{\Sigma gC^2}{n{=}2}} \times \text{Col.10}$
			C	g	n	$= (\text{Col.3})^2$	$= (\text{Col.4}) \times (\text{Col.6})$				
1	34										
2	34 1/8	+ 1/8	+1/8	3	3	1/64	3/64				
3	34 1/4	+ 1/8	-1/8	1	4	1/64	1/64				
4	34 1/8	- 1/8	-1/4	2	6	1/16	2/16				
5	34 1/4	+ 1/8	+1/2	1	7	1/4	1/4				
6	35	+ 3/4	-1/2	1	8	1/4	1/4				
7	34 3/4	- 1/4	+3/4	1	9	9/16	9/16				
8	35 1/4	+ 1/2	+1	2	11	1	2				
9	36 1/4	+ 1	+1 1/2	2	13	9/4	9/2				
10	36	- 1/4									
11	37 1/2	+ 1 1/2									
12	37	- 1/2									
13	38	+ 1									
	39 1/2	+ 1 1/2									
								7 3/4	6/10	77/100	1 54/100

SYSTEM 78

WILDER'S MODIFIED RELATIVE STRENGTH INDEX

SYSTEM DEFINITIONS:

(1)   Col. 1 is the daily high price.

(2)   Col. 2 is the daily low price.

(3)   Col. 3 is the average of high and low price.

(4)   Col. 4 is the 7 day exponentially smoothed moving average of Col. 3.

(5)   In Col. 4, compare the current moving average value with the previous moving average value.
If the moving average value is positive, put in Col. 5.
If the moving average value is negative, put in Col. 6.

(6)   Add first seven prices in Col. 5, divide by 7 and put in Col. 7.
Then,

$$\text{Current 7 day up value} = \frac{\text{Previous 7 day up value(Col.7)} \times 6 + \text{Current value (Col. 5)}}{7}$$

(7)   Add first seven prices in Col. 6, divide by 7 and put in Col. 8. Then,

$$\text{Current 7 day down value} = \frac{\text{Previous 7 day down value(Col.8)} \times 6 + \text{Current value (Col. 6)}}{7}$$

(8) $\text{Col. 9} = \dfrac{\text{Col.7 (7 day up value)}}{\text{Col.8 (7 day down value)}}$

(9)   Col. 10 = Col. 9 + 1

(10) $\text{Col. 11} = \dfrac{100}{\text{Col.10}}$

(11) Col. 12 = 100 – Col.11 = Relative strength Index (RSI)

(12) Sell signal is generated when the top (Highest value) declines by 5%.

(13) Buy signal is generated when the bottom (Lowest Value) rises by 5%.

(14) Once a Buy or Sell signal is generated, the old position is liquidated simultaneously. In other words, the system is always in the market.

(15) This is a completely mechanical method using triple filters.

WORK SHEET

SYSTEM 78

WILDER'S MODIFIED RELATIVE STRENGTH INDEX

	1	2	3	4	5	6	7	8	9	10	11	12
	Daily High Price	Daily Low Price	Avg.of High & Low	7 day Expn smooth moving Avg.of Col. 3	Up Value	Down Value	7 day up value	7 day down value	$=\frac{7}{8}$	$=9+1$	$=\frac{100}{10}$	$=100-11$
1	62.75	62.00	62.38	62.71								
2	63.50	63.00	63.25	62.85	0	.11						
3	64.00	63.00	63.50	63.01	.14	0						
4	63.50	62.50	63.00	63.01	.16	0						
5	63.00	62.00	62.50	62.88	0	0						
6	63.25	62.75	63.00	62.91	.03	.13						
7	63.00	62.00	62.50	62.81	0	0	.05	.05	1.00	2.00	50.00	50.00
8	63.25	62.00	62.63	62.76	0	.10	.04	.05	.80	1.80	55.56	44.44
9	64.00	63.00	63.50	62.95	.19	.05	.06	.05	1.20	2.20	45.45	54.55
10	65.00	64.50	64.75	63.40	.45	0	.12	.05	2.40	3.40	29.41	70.59
11	65.50	64.00	64.75	63.74	.34	0	.15	.05	3.00	4.00	25.00	75.00
12	65.00	64.50	64.75	63.99	.25	0	.16	.05	3.20	4.20	23.81	76.19
13	66.00	65.00	65.50	64.37	.38	0	.20	.05	4.00	5.00	20.00	80.00
14	66.50	65.50	66.00	64.78	.41	0	.23	.05	4.60	5.60	17.86	82.14
15	67.00	66.00	66.50	65.21	.43	0	.26	.05	5.20	6.20	16.13	83.87
16	66.50	66.00	66.25	65.47	.26	0	.26	.05	5.20	6.20	16.13	83.87
17	67.00	66.00	66.50	65.73	.26	0	.26	.05	5.20	6.20	16.13	83.87
18	68.00	67.00	67.50	66.17	.44	0	.28	.05	5.60	6.60	15.15	84.85

WILDER'S MODIFIED RELATIVE STRENGTH INDEX

WORK SHEET
SYSTEM 78

Day	1 — Daily High Price	2 — Daily Low Price	3 — Avg. of High & Low	4 — 7 day Expn smooth moving Avg. of Col. 3	5 — Up Value	6 — Down Value	7 — 7 day up value	8 — 7 day down value	9 — $\frac{7}{8}$	10 — $= 9 + 1$	11 — $= \frac{100}{10}$	12 — $= 100 - 11$
19	68.00	67.50	67.75	66.56	.39	0	.31	.05	6.20	7.20	13.89	86.11
20	68.50	67.50	68.00	66.92	.36	0	.32	.05	6.40	7.40	13.51	86.49
21	68.00	67.50	67.75	67.13	.21	0	.31	.05	6.20	7.20	13.89	86.11
22	67.50	67.00	67.25	67.16	0	.21	.27	.05	5.40	6.40	15.63	84.38
23	(67.50)	66.00	66.50	66.99	0	0	.24	.07	3.43	4.43	22.08	(77.42)
24	65.00	64.00	64.50	66.37	0	.17	.21	.15	1.40	2.40	41.67	58.33
25	63.00	62.00	62.50	65.40	0	.62	.18	.26	.69	1.69	59.09	40.91
26	62.00	61.00	61.50	64.43	0	.97	.16	.36	.44	1.44	69.23	30.77
27	60.00	59.00	59.50	63.20	0	.97	.14	.49	.29	1.29	77.28	22.22
28	60.00	57.00	58.50	62.02	0	1.23	.13	.59	.22	1.22	81.94	18.06
29	59.00	58.00	58.50	61.14	0	1.18	.11	.63	.17	1.17	85.14	14.86
30	60.00	59.00	59.50	60.73	0	.88	.10	.60	.17	1.17	85.71	14.29
31	61.00	(60.00)	60.50	60.67	0	.41	.09	.52	.17	1.17	85.25	14.75
32	62.00	61.00	61.50	60.88	.21	.06	.11	.48	.23	1.23	81.36	(18.64)

Annotations (right margin of Column 12): Top — Sell (77.42); Bottom — Buy (18.64)

180

WILDER'S VOLATILITY SYSTEM

GENERAL THEORY AND DISCUSSION:

(1)   Range is directly proportional to volatility. Higher the range, higher the volatility and vice versa.

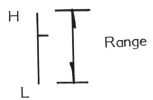

(2)   True Range (TR) is defined as the greatest of the following.

(a)   The Distance from today's high to low.

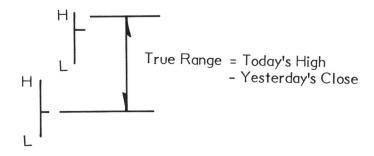

(b)   The distance from yesterday's close to today's high.

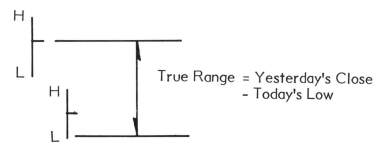

(c)   The distance from yesterday's close to today's low.

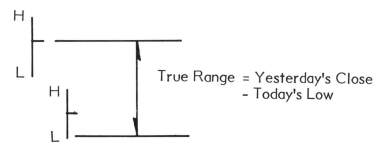

(3)   Average True Range (ATR) is initially obtained by adding the true ranges for 7 days or weeks and dividing by 7.

(4)   Current ATR = $\dfrac{\text{Previous ATR} \times 6 + \text{Current True Range (TR)}}{7}$

(5)   Average Range constant (ARC) = ATR x C where
       C = Constant between 1 and 3.1.

       For most stocks on weekly basis C $\simeq$ 1

       For most commodities on daily basis C $\simeq$ 3

       Experiment a little bit to find right constant C for your work.

(6)   (a)   For initial entry during downtrend (as defined in system 47), circle the closing price each time a new lower close is made.

       (b)   We are looking for the time to go long.

       (c)   Stop and reverse (SAR) for next week is calculated by adding this week's ARC to the lowest close.

              e.g. SAR for line 10 = Lowest close + ARC for line 9
                                   = 35.13 + 2.43
                                   = 37.56

       (d)   When current closing price rises above SAR, a Buy Signal is generated.

(7)   (a)   For initial entry during uptrend (as defined in system 47), circle the closing price each time a new higher close is made.

       (b)   We are looking for an entry to sell short.

       (c)   SAR for next week is calculated by subtracting this week's ARC from highest close.

              e.g. SAR for line 15 = Highest close - ARC for line 14.
                                   = 37.75 - 2.04
                                   = 35.71

       (d)   When current closing price falls below SAR, a sell signal is generated.

SYSTEM DEFINITIONS:

(1)   Col. 1 is the weekly High Price.

(2)   Col. 2 is the weekly low price.

(3)   Col. 3 is the weekly close price.

(4)   Col. 4 is the true range.

(5)   To start, Add first seven figures in Col. 4, divide by 7 and put in Col. 5. Then,

$$\text{Current ATR} = \frac{\text{Previous ATR x 6 + Current True Range (TR)}}{7}$$

(6)   Initial entry during uptrend and downtrend is explained above.

(7)   Once a Buy signal is generated,

    (a)   Circle each time a new higher close is made.

    (b)   SAR for Next Week = Highest close - This week's ARC

    (c)   Sell signal is generated, when the current closing price falls below SAR.

(8)   After a sell signal is generated,

    (a)   Circle each time a new lower close is made.

    (b)   SAR for Next week = Lowest close + This week's ARC.

    (c)   Buy signal is generated, when the current closing price rises above SAR.

(9)   Once a Buy or Sell signal is generated, the old position is liquidated simultaneously. In other words, the system is always in the market.

(10)   Completely Mechanical Method.

WORK SHEET

SYSTEM 79

WILDER'S VOLATILITY SYSTEM

	1	2	3	4	5	6	7	
	Weekly High Price	Weekly Low Price	Weekly Close Price	True Range (TR)	7 Week Average True Range (ATR)	Average Range Constant (ARC)	Stop and Reverse (SAR)	
1	36.50	35.00	36.00					
2	37.00	35.50	36.50	1.50				
3	37.75	36.00	37.25	1.75				
4	38.00	37.00	37.50	1.00				
5	38.33	36.17	38.08	2.16				
6	39.08	36.83	37.17	2.25				
7	39.25	37.00	39.00	2.25				
8	40.50	35.38	36.75	5.12	2.29	2.29		
9	38.25	35.00	35.13	3.25	2.43	2.43	39.04	
10	37.63	33.88	36.00	3.75	2.62	2.62	37.56	
11	36.50	34.63	36.25	1.87	2.51	2.51	37.75	
12	36.00	35.50	35.75	0.75	2.26	2.26	37.64	
13	36.38	35.75	35.75	0.63	2.03	2.03	37.39	
14	37.75	35.63	37.75	2.12	2.04	2.04	37.16	Buy
15	39.38	37.50	38.25	1.88	2.02	2.02	35.71	
16	38.13	34.88	35.00	3.37	2.21	2.21	36.23	Sell
17	35.63	33.00	35.50	2.63	2.27	2.27	37.21	
18	36.00	34.38	35.00	1.62	2.18	2.18	37.27	
19	36.75	34.13	36.38	2.62	2.24	2.24	37.18	
20	36.88	35.63	36.50	1.25	2.10	2.10	37.24	
21	37.00	35.75	36.25	1.25	1.98	1.98	37.10	
22	37.50	35.50	36.75	2.00	1.98	1.98	36.98	
23	36.75	35.00	36.00	1.75	1.95	1.95	36.98	
24	36.00	34.75	35.00	1.25	1.85	1.85	36.95	
25	35.00	33.25	34.50	1.75	1.83	1.83	36.85	
26	33.00	32.25	32.75	2.25	1.89	1.89	36.33	
27	33.25	33.00	33.00	0.50	1.69	1.69	34.64	
28	34.50	33.50	34.25	1.50	1.67	1.67	34.44	
29	35.00	34.25	34.50	0.75	1.54	1.54	34.42	Buy

SYSTEM 80

TREND BY ZERO BALANCE

(1)   Developer is unknown.

(2)   Generates the direction of the trend (defined later on in the system).

(3)   Trade only in the direction of the trend, i.e., if the trend is up, trade long and if the trend is down trade short.

(4)   Identify seven or eight significant Tops and Bottoms (as defined in system 47) on your bar chart.

(5)   Label your bar chart with A, B, C, D, E and F marking the most recent Top or Bottom as A and going backward.

(6) $A^1 = C + D - F.$

(7) A^1 is the zero balance line point which will fall directly above or below A.

(8)   If A is above A^1, the trend is up.

(9)   If A is below A^1, the trend is down.

(10) $A^{1+} = B + C - E.$ A^{1+} balance point will give you the price objective of the current swing.

(11)   Projected zero balance line normally has zig zag patterns.

(12)   If projected zero balance line is straight up or down, the market is in over-extended position subject to sharp reversal.

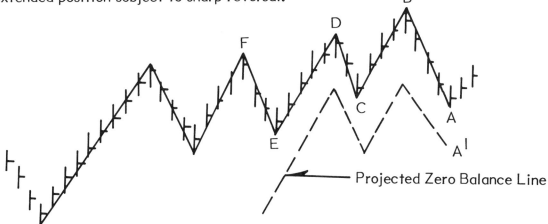

Projected Zero Balance Line

A = 36.75 B = 37.00 C = 35.00 D = 36.00 E = 34.00 F = 35.00

$A^1 = C + D - F = 35.00 + 36.00 - 35.00 = 36.00$

Since A is above A^1, the trend is up.

$A^{1+} = B + C - E = 37.00 + 35.00 - 34.00 = 38.00$

Price objective of current swing is 38.00

185

SYSTEM 81

EASY RELATIVE STRENGTH METHOD

COMMODITY TRADERS:

(1)   Find the % price change between this week's closing price and closing price five weeks ago for all commodities.

(2)   Arrange commodities from top to bottom using Relative Strength analysis, i.e.,commodity with highest % price change is 1 and the commodity with lowest % price change is last.

(3)   Buy the commodity in the top 10%. When the commodity drops below 10%, sell it and switch into new commodity that is rising above the top 10% line.

(4)   Sell short the commodity in the bottom 10%. When the commodity rises above the bottom 10% line, cover your short position and switch into new commodity that is falling below bottom 10% line.

STOCK/OPTION TRADERS:

(1)   Find the % price change between this week's closing price and closing price nine weeks ago for all your selected stocks.

(2)   Arrange the stocks from top to bottom using Relative Strength analysis, i.e.,the stock with highest % price change is 1 and the stock with lowest % price change is last.

(3)   Buy the stock in the top 10%. When the stock drops below top 10%, sell it and switch into new stock that is rising above the top 10% line.

(4)   Sell short the stock in the bottom 10%. When the stock rises above your bottom 10% line, cover your short position and switch into new stock that is falling below bottom 10% line.

Note: You can vary the time period according to your taste.

SYSTEM 82

ANGULAR THEORY OF PRICE TRENDS

(1)   Work with major trend and define major low and major high.

(2)   <u>During Downtrend,</u>

   (a)   Draw a line AB passing through major low (A) and preceding major high (B).

   (b)   The angle this line AB makes with the horizontal is known as principal angle.

   (c)   Complementary angle = 90° - principal angle

   (d)   Draw a line AC making this complementary angle with the horizontal.

   (e)   This complementary angle usually determines the future direction of the uptrend.

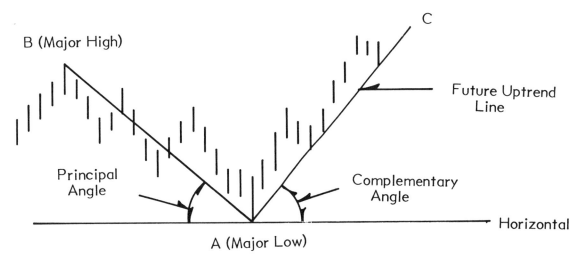

(3)   <u>During Uptrend:</u>

   (a)   Draw a line ED passing through major high (D) and the preceding major low (E).

   (b)   The angle this line makes with the horizontal is known as Principal Angle.

   (c)   Complementary Angle = 90° - Principal Angle.

   (d)   Draw a line DF making this complementary angle with the horizontal.

(e) This Complementary angle usually determines the future direction of the downtrend.

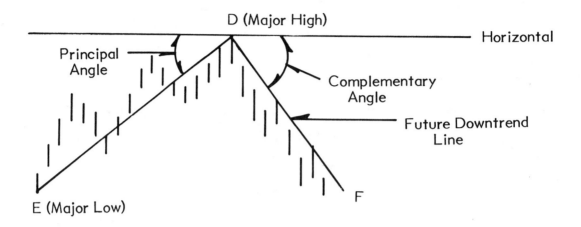

(4) As a general rule, the larger the principal angle employed, the shorter its applicability; the smaller the principal angle, the greater its applicability.

APPENDIX

ABBREVIATIONS

+	Positive
-	Negative
0	Zero
5-DH	5 Day High
5-DL	5 Day Low
Avg	Average
ATR	Average True Range
ARC	Average Range Constant
B	Buy
C	Close
CPR	Closing Price Reversal
CSC	Cumulative Smoothing Constant
ESMA	Exponentially Smoothed Moving Average
Expn	Exponentially
H	High
(HLC) Avg	Average of High, Low and Close
I	Intersection
IR	Inside Range
L	Low
LSWMA	Linearly Step Weighted Moving Average
MA	Moving Average
ML	Median Line
ML2-3	Median Line Passing through pivots 2 and 3
NR	Narrow Range
O	Opening Price
OBV	On Balance Volume
PB	Penetration of Bottom
PT	Penetration of Top
R	Range = High - Low
RC1	% Rate of Change 1 Day, Week or Unit Ago
RCn	% Rate of Change n Days, Weeks or Units Ago
RSI	Relative Strength Index
S	Sell

SAR	Stop and Reverse
SMA	Simple Moving Average
SRL	Speed Resistance Line
SWMA	Step Weighted Moving Average
T	Top
TOB	Test of Bottom
TOT	Test of Top
TR	True Range
V	Volume
WMA	Week Moving Average

APPLICATION GUIDE

System	Commodity Trend		Short/Intermediate Term Stock Trend	Long Term Stock Trend
1	(a) Daily Closing Prices		(a) Weekly Closing Prices	(a) Weekly Closing Prices
	(b) Single MA Time period in days		(b) 10 Week simple MA	(b) 30 Week simple MA
	Cocoa	55		
	Corn	50		
	Sugar	64		
	Cotton	65		
	Silver	30		
	Copper	68		
	Soybeans	55		
	Soybean Meal	55		
	Wheat	50		
	Pork Bellies	22		
	Soybean Oil	55		
	Plywood	65		
	Live Hogs	25		
	Live Cattle	33		
2	(a) Daily Closing Prices		(a) Weekly Closing Prices	(a) Weekly Closing Prices
	(b) Moving Avg. Time Period as discussed in System 1		(b) 10 Week ESMA	(b) 30 Week ESMA
	(c) Use ESMA			
3	(a) Daily Closing Prices		(a) Weekly Closing Prices	(a) Weekly Closing Prices
	(b) Moving Avg. Time Period as discussed in System 1		(b) 10 Week SWMA	(b) 30 Week SWMA
	(c) Use SWMA			

System	Commodity Trend	Short/Intermediate Term Stock Trend	Long Term Stock Trend
4	(a) Daily Closing Prices	(a) Weekly Closing Prices	(a) Weekly Closing Prices
	(b) Moving Avg. Time Period as discussed in System I	(b) 10 Week L SWMA	(b) 30 Week L SWMA
	(c) Use L SWMA		
5	(a) Daily Closing Prices	(a) Weekly Closing Prices	(a) Weekly Closing Prices
	(b) MA Time period as discussed in System I with 5 day time filter	(b) 10 Week MA with 2 Week time filter	(b) 30 Week MA with 4 Week time filter
6	(a) Daily Closing Prices	(b) Weekly Closing Prices	(a) Weekly Closing Prices
	(b) MA Time period as discussed in System I	(b) 10 Week MA	(b) 30 Week MA
	(c) 6% for below $20 5% for $20 to $39 4% for $40 to $59 3% for $60 to $199 2% for over $200	(c) 6% for below $20 5% for $20 to $39 4% for $40 to $59 3% for $60 to $199 2% for over $200	(c) 6% for below $20 5% for $20 to $39 4% for $40 to $59 3% for $60 to $199 2% for over $200
7	(a) Daily Closing Prices	(a) Weekly Closing Prices	(a) Weekly Closing Prices
	(b) MA Time period as discussed in System I	(b) 10 Week MA	(b) 30 Week MA
	(c) Round off Time period in days to week	(c) 6 Week Volatility	(c) 10 Week Volatility
	(d) Use this Time period in Weeks as Volatility filter		

System	Commodity Trend	Short/Intermediate Term Stock Trend	Long Term Stock Trend
8	(a) Combine System 5 & 6	(a) Combine System 5 & 6	(a) Combine System 5 & 6
9	(a) Daily Closing Prices	(a) Weekly Closing Prices	(a) Weekly Closing Prices
	(b) 20 Day Moving Avg with 10 day Lag	(b) 10 Week Moving Avg with 5 week Lag	(b) 30 Week Moving Avg with 15 week Lag
10	(a) Daily Closing Prices	(a) Weekly Closing Prices	(a) Weekly Closing Prices
	(b) 20 day MA	(b) 10 Week MA	(b) 30 Week MA
	(c) 3 Day Lead	(c) One Week Lead	(c) 4 Week Lead
11	(a) As discussed using Daily Bar Chart	(a) As discussed using Weekly Bar Chart	(a) As discussed using Monthly Bar Chart
12	(a) Daily Closing Prices	(a) Weekly Closing Prices	(a) Weekly Closing Prices
	(b) n day single Moving Avg Time period	(b) 10 Week MA	(b) 30 Week MA
	(c) Smoothing Constant $= \dfrac{2}{n+1}$	(c) Smoothing Constant $= \dfrac{2}{n+1} = 0.18$	(c) Smoothing Constant $= \dfrac{2}{31} = .064$
	(d) Additional Smoothing Constant = .003	(d) Additional Smoothing Constant = .003	(d) Additional Smoothing Constant = .003
	(e) Max CSC $= \dfrac{2}{n+1} + .03$	(e) Max CSC $= .18 + .03 = .21$	(e) Max CSC $= .064 + .03$ $= .094$

System	Commodity Trend		Short/Intermediate Term Stock Trend	Long Term Stock Trend
13	(a)	Daily Closing Prices	(a) Weekly Closing Prices	(a) Weekly Closing Prices
	(b)	Two Moving Average Time period in days	(b) 4 Week MA (faster) 10 Week MA (slower)	(b) 8 Week MA (faster) 30 Week MA (slower)
	Cocoa	7,25		
	Corn	11,47		
	Sugar	5,50		
	Cotton	16,25		
	Silver	4,26		
	Copper	17,33		
	Soybeans	16,50		
	Soybean Meal	18,50		
	Wheat	11,47		
	Pork Bellies	25,46		
	Soybean Oil	14,50		
	Plywood	24,42		
	Live Hogs	3,14		
	Ginnie Maes	4,36		
	T-Bills	6,18		
	Gold	14,50		
14	(a)	Daily Closing Prices	(a) Weekly Closing Prices	(a) Weekly Closing Prices
	(b)	10 Day Moving Avg.	(b) 5 Week MA	(b) 15 Week MA
		20 Day Moving Avg.	10 Week MA	30 Week MA

System		Commodity Trend	Short/Intermediate Term Stock Trend	Long Term Stock Trend
15	(a)	Daily Closing Prices	(a) Weekly Closing Prices	(a) Weekly Closing Prices
	(b)	10 Day MA	(b) 5 Week MA	(b) 12 Week MA
		20 Day MA	10 Week MA	24 Week MA
		40 Day MA	20 Week MA	48 Week MA
16	(a)	Daily Closing Prices	(a) Weekly Closing Prices	(a) Weekly Closing Prices
	(b)	10 Day MA	(b) 5 Week MA	(b) 12 Week MA
		20 Day MA	10 Week MA	24 Week MA
		40 Day MA	20 Week MA	48 Week MA
17	(a)	General Discussion on Moving Average Systems	(a) General Discussion on Moving Average Systems	(a) General Discussion on Moving Average Systems
18	(a)	Practical Applications of Moving Averages	(a) Practical Applications of Moving Averages	(a) Practical Applications of Moving Averages
19	(a)	Daily Prices and Volumes	(a) Weekly Prices and Volumes	(a) Weekly Prices and Volumes
	(b)	20 Day MA	(b) 10 Week MA	(b) 30 Week MA
20	(a)	Daily Prices and Volumes	(a) Weekly Prices and Volumes	(a) Weekly Prices and Volumes
	(b)	20 Day MA	(b) 10 Week MA	(b) 30 Week MA
21	(a)	Daily Prices and Volumes	(a) Weekly Prices and Volumes	(a) Weekly Prices and Volumes
	(b)	20 Day MA	(b) 10 Week MA	(b) 30 Week MA

System	Commodity Trend	Short/Intermediate Term Stock Trend	Long Term Stock Trend
22	Not Applicable	As Discussed	As Discussed
23	(a) Daily Prices and Volumes	(a) Weekly Prices and Volumes	(a) Weekly Prices and Volumes
	(b) 20 Day MA	(b) 10 Week MA	(b) 30 Week MA
24	(a) Daily Prices and Volumes	(a) Weekly Prices and Volumes	(a) Weekly Prices and Volumes
	(b) 20 Day MA	(b) 10 Week MA	(b) 30 Week MA
25	(a) Not Applicable	(a) As Discussed	(a) As Discussed
26	(a) Daily Prices and Volumes	(a) Weekly Prices and Volumes	(a) Monthly Prices and Volumes
27	(a) Daily Prices and Volumes	(a) As Discussed	(a) Weekly Prices and Volumes
	(b) 20 Day MA 8 Day MA		(b) 30 Week MA 8 Week MA
28	(a) Daily Prices and Volumes	(a) Weekly Prices and Volumes	(a) Monthly Prices and Volumes
29	(a) Daily Prices and Volumes	(a) Weekly Prices and Volumes	(a) Monthly Prices and Volumes
30	(a) Daily Prices and Volumes	(a) Weekly Prices and Volumes	(a) Monthly Prices and Volumes
31	(a) General Discussion on Volume systems	(a) General Discussion on Volume systems	(a) General Discussion on Volume systems

System	Commodity Trend	Short/Intermediate Term Stock Trend	Long Term Stock Trend
32	(a) Daily Prices RC5	(a) Weekly Prices RC2	(a) Weekly Prices RC4
33	(a) Daily Prices RC5 + RC10	(a) Weekly Prices RC2 + RC5	(a) Weekly Prices RC4 + RC10
34	(a) Daily Prices RC5 + RC10 + RC15	(a) Weekly Prices RC2 + RC5 + RC8	(a) Weekly Prices RC4 + RC10 + RC16
35	(a) Daily Prices RC5 + RC10 + RC15 + RC20	(a) Weekly Prices RC2 + RC5 + RC8 + RC11	(a) Weekly Prices RC4 + RC10 + RC16 + RC22
36	(a) Daily Prices	Same as Discussed	(a) Weekly Prices
	(b) RC10		(b) RC13
	(c) 6 Day ESMA of RC10		(c) 8 Week ESMA of RC13
37	(a) Daily Closing Prices	Same as Discussed	(a) Weekly Closing Prices
	(b) 20 Day ESMA		(b) 30 Week ESMA
	(c) RC10		(c) RC15
	(d) RC10		(d) RC15
38	(a) Daily Closing Prices	(a) Weekly Closing Prices	(a) Weekly Closing Prices
	(b) RC10	(b) RC5	(b) RC13
	(c) RC10	(c) RC5	(c) RC13

System	Commodity Trend	Short/Intermediate Term Stock Trend	Long Term Stock Trend
39	(a) Daily Closing Prices	(a) Weekly Closing Prices	(a) Weekly Closing Prices
	(b) 20 Day MA RC4	(b) 10 Week MA RC2	(b) 20 Week MA RC4
40	(a) Daily Closing Prices	(a) Weekly Closing Prices	(a) Weekly Closing Prices
	(b) 20 Day MA RC4 + RC8	(b) 10 Week MA RC2 + RC4	(b) 20 Week MA RC4 + RC8
41	(a) Daily Closing Prices	(a) Weekly Closing Prices	(a) Weekly Closing Prices
	(b) 20 Day MA RC4 + RC8 + RC12	(b) 10 Week MA RC2 + RC4 + RC6	(b) 20 Week MA RC4 + RC8 + RC12
42	(a) Daily Closing Prices	(a) Weekly Closing Prices	(a) Weekly Closing Prices
	(b) 20 Day MA RC4 + RC8 + RC12 + RC16	(b) 10 Week MA RC2 + RC4 + RC6 + RC8	(b) 20 Week MA RC4 + RC8 + RC12 + RC16
43	(a) Daily Closing Prices	(a) Weekly Closing Prices	(a) Weekly Closing Prices
	(b) 10 Day MA, RC5	(b) 3 Week MA, RC2	(b) 10 Week MA, RC5
44	(a) Daily Closing Prices	(a) Weekly Closing Prices	(a) Weekly Closing Prices
	(b) 10 Day MA, RC5	(b) 3 Week MA, RC2	(b) 10 Week MA, RC5
	(c) 15 Day MA, RC8	(c) 6 Week MA, RC4	(c) 20 Week MA, RC10
45	(a) Daily Closing Prices	(a) Weekly Closing Prices	(a) Weekly Closing Prices
	(b) 10 day MA, RC5	(b) 3 Week MA, RC2	(b) 10 Week MA, RC5
	(c) 15 Day MA, RC8	(c) 6 Week MA, RC4	(c) 20 Week MA, RC10
	(d) 20 Day MA, RC11	(d) 9 Week MA, RC6	(d) 30 Week MA, RC15

System	Commodity Trend	Short/Intermediate Term Stock Trend	Long Term Stock Trend
46	(a) Daily Closing Prices	(a) Weekly Closing Prices	(a) Weekly Closing Prices
	(b) 10 Day MA, RC5	(b) 3 Week MA, RC2	(b) 10 Week MA, RC5
	(c) 15 Day MA, RC8	(c) 6 Week MA, RC4	(c) 20 Week MA, RC10
	(d) 20 Day MA, RC11	(d) 9 Week MA, RC6	(d) 30 Week MA, RC15
	(e) 25 Day MA, RC14	(e) 12 Week MA, RC8	(e) 40 Week MA, RC20
47	(a) Daily Bar Chart	(a) Weekly Bar Chart	(a) Monthly Bar Chart
48	(a) Daily Bar Chart	(a) Weekly Bar Chart	(a) Monthly Bar Chart
49	(a) Daily Prices	(a) Weekly Prices	(a) Weekly Prices
50	As Discussed	Not Applicable	Not Applicable
51	As Discussed	Not Applicable	Not Applicable
52	As Discussed	Not Applicable	Not Applicable
53	As Discussed	Not Applicable	Not Applicable
54	As Discussed	Not Applicable	Not Applicable
55	As Discussed	Not Applicable	Not Applicable
56	As Discussed	Not Applicable	Not Applicable
57	As Discussed	Not Applicable	Not Applicable
58	Not Applicable, Use 7 Week channel for Copper	As Discussed	As Discussed

System	Commodity Trend	Short/Intermediate Term Stock Trend	Long Term Stock Trend
59	Not Applicable, Use 7 Week modified channel for Copper	As Discussed	As Discussed
60	Daily Bar Chart	Weekly Bar Chart	Monthly Bar Chart
61	Daily Bar Chart	Weekly Bar Chart	Monthly Bar Chart
62	Daily Bar Chart	Weekly Bar Chart	Monthly Bar Chart
63	As Discussed	Monthly Price	Not Applicable
64	Daily Bar Chart	Weekly Bar Chart with 3 previous closing prices	Monthly Bar Chart with 2 previous closing prices
65	Daily Prices	Weekly Prices	Monthly Prices
66	Daily Prices	Weekly Prices	Monthly Prices
67	(a) Daily Closing Prices (b) 10 Day MA (c) 20 Day MA (d) 10 Day Moving Total	As Discussed	(a) Weekly Closing Prices (b) 10 Week MA (c) 20 Week MA (d) 5 Week Moving Total
68	(a) Daily Closing Prices (b) 10 Day MA (c) 20 Day MA (d) 40 Day MA (e) 10 Day Moving Total	As Discussed	(a) Weekly Closing Prices (b) 10 Week MA (c) 20 Week MA (d) 40 Week MA (e) 10 Week Moving Total

System	Commodity Trend	Short/Intermediate Term Stock Trend	Long Term Stock Trend
69	(a) Daily Closing Prices	(a) Weekly Closing Prices	(a) Weekly Closing Prices
	(b) 10 Day MA	(b) 5 Week MA	(b) 10 Week MA
	(c) RC5	(c) RC3	(c) RC5
	(d) 10 Day MA	(d) 5 Week MA	(d) 10 Week MA
70	(a) Daily Closing Prices	(a) Weekly Closing Prices	(a) Weekly Closing Prices
	(b) 10 Day and 20 Day MA	(b) 5 Week and 10 Week MA	(b) 15 Week and 30 Week MA
	(c) RC5	(c) RC3	(c) RC8
71	(a) Daily Closing Prices	(a) Weekly Closing Prices	(a) Weekly Closing Prices
	(b) 10 Day, 20 Day and 40 Day MA	(b) 5 Week, 10 Week and 15 Week MA	(b) 15 Week, 30 Week and 45 Week MA
	(c) RC8	(c) RC3	(c) RC8
	(d) 10 Day MA	(d) 7 Week MA	(d) 7 Week MA
72	(a) Daily Closing Prices	As Discussed	(a) Weekly Closing Prices
	(b) RC10		(b) RC15
	(c) 10 Day MA		(c) 15 Week MA
73	(a) Daily Prices	(a) Weekly Prices	(a) Monthly Prices
74	(a) Daily Prices	(a) Weekly Prices	(a) Monthly Prices
75	(a) Daily Prices	(a) Not Applicable	(a) Weekly Prices

System	Commodity Trend	Short/Intermediate Term Stock Trend	Long Term Stock Trend
76	Not Applicable	As Discussed	Not Applicable
77	Daily Closing Prices	Weekly Closing Prices	Monthly Closing Prices
78	As Discussed	Weekly Prices 7 Week MA, 7 Week up and down	Weekly Prices 14 Week MA, 14 Week up and down
79	Daily Prices	Weekly Prices	Monthly Prices
80	Daily Bar Chart	Weekly Bar Chart	Monthly Bar Chart
81	As Discussed	As Discussed	% Price Change 20 Weeks ago
82	Daily Bar Chart	Weekly Bar Chart	Monthly Bar Chart

TRADERS PRESS, INC.®
INCORPORATED
P.O. BOX 6206
GREENVILLE, S.C. 29606

Books and Gifts
for Investors and Traders

A Complete Guide to Trading Profits (Paris)
Beginner's Guide to Computer Assisted Trading (Alexander)
Chart Reading for Professional Traders (Jenkins)
Commodity Spreads: Analysis, Selection and Trading Techniques (Smith)
Comparison of Twelve Technical Trading Systems (Lukac, Brorsen, & Irwin)
Day Trading with Short Term Price Patterns and Opening Range Breakout (Crabel)
Fibonacci Ratios with Pattern Recognition (Pesavento)
Geometry of Stock Market Profits (Jenkins)
Harmonic Vibrations (Pesavento)
How to Trade in Stocks (Livermore)
Jesse Livermore: Speculator-King (Sarnoff)
Magic of Moving Averages (Lowry)
Planetary Harmonics of Speculative Markets (Pesavento)
Point & Figure Charting (Aby)
Point & Figure Charting: Commodity and Stock Trading Techniques (Zieg)
Profitable Grain Trading (Ainsworth)
Reminiscences of A Stock Operator (Lefevre)
Stock Market Trading Systems (Appel & Hitschler)
Stock Patterns for Day Trading (Rudd)
Study Helps in Point and Figure Technique (Wheelan)
Technically Speaking (Wilkinson)
The Professional Commodity Trader (Kroll)
The Taylor Trading Technique (Taylor)
The Traders (Kleinfeld)
The Trading Rule That Can Make You Rich* (Dobson)
Traders Guide to Technical Analysis (Hardy)
Trading Secrets of the Inner Circle (Goodwin)
Trading S&P Futures and Options (Lloyd)
Understanding Andrews Pitchfork (Schuler & Dobson)
Understanding Bollinger Bands (Dobson)
Understanding Fibonacci Numbers (Dobson)
Viewpoints of a Commodity Trader (Longstreet)
Wall Street Ventures & Adventures through Forty Years (Wyckoff)
Winning Market Systems (Appel)

Please write or call for our current catalog describing these and many other books and gifts of interest to
investors and traders

1-800-927-8222   FAX 864-298-0221
Tradersprs@aol.com
http://www.traderspress.com

◆TECHNICAL ANALYSIS ◆OPTIONS ◆TRADING PSYCHOLOGY & DISCIPLINE ◆SPREAD TRADING
◆ELLIOTT WAVE ◆W.D. GANN ◆INTRADAY TRADING
◆TRADING STRATEGIES◆

FREE TRADERS CATALOG

◆FIBONACCI ◆FLOOR TRADING ◆FREE BOOKS (WITH ADDITIONAL PURCHASE) ◆MONEY MANAGEMENT
◆MUTUAL FUNDS ◆SHORT SELLING/BEAR MARKETS ◆STOCK INDEX TRADING ◆SYSTEMS & METHODS ◆MANY
OTHER TOPICS◆

TRADERS PRESS, INC. publishes a 100 page catalog which lists and describes
hundreds of books, tapes, courses and gifts of interest to stock, options, and futures
traders.

(Regular price $10)

Get a free copy by contacting
TRADERS PRESS, INC.
PO BOX 6206
GREENVILLE, SC 29606

_____

Serving traders since 1975

800-927-8222
864-298-0222
FAX 864-298-0221
Tradersprs@aol.com
http://www.traderspress.com

Visit our Website at http://www.traderspress.com

• View our latest releases
• Browse our updated catalog
• Access our Gift Shop for investors
• Read our book reviews

Contact us for our hardcopy 100 page catalog.

TRADERS PRESS, INC.™
PO Box 6206
Greenville, SC 29606

Tradersprs@aol.com

800-927-8222

Fax 864-298-0221